GCSE English

Frankenstein

by Mary Shelley

Frankenstein — it's a very tall story about a very tall monster.
But unfortunately, that won't get you very far in your GCSE essays.

Not to worry. This brilliant Text Guide explains the whole novel —
characters, language, themes, historical background... the lot. And because
it's a CGP book, we get straight to the point, with no needless rambling.

We've also included plenty of practice questions to test you on what you've
learned, plus advice on how to plan and write top-grade answers in the exam!

The Text Guide

CONTENTS

CONTENTS

Section Four — Themes

Section Five — Writer's Techniques

Section Six — Exam Advice

Published by CGP

Editors:
Emma Bonney
David Broadbent
Emma Crighton

Contributor:
Nicola Woodfin

With thanks to Matt Topping and Elisabeth Quincey for the proofreading,
and Jan Greenway for the copyright research.

Acknowledgements:
Cover Illustration and image on page 4 by Ricardo Sandoval
With thanks to Rex Features for permission to use the images on pages 3, 4, 5, 10, 11, 12, 13, 15, 16, 17, 18, 20, 24, 25, 27, 28, 29, 30, 31, 32, 33, 36, 38, 39, 40, 41, 42, 47, 48, 49, 50 & 52
With thanks to iStockphoto.com for permission to use the images on pages 3 & 46
With thanks to Mary Evans Picture Library for permission to use the images on pages 1, 2, 6, 7 & 8
With thanks to Kobal for permission to use the image on page 19
With thanks to ArenaPAL.com for permission to use the images on pages 14, 21, 26, 37 & 51

ISBN: 978 1 78294 312 9
Printed by Elanders Ltd, Newcastle upon Tyne.
Clipart from Corel®

Based on the classic CGP style created by Richard Parsons.

Introducing 'Frankenstein' and Mary Shelley

'Frankenstein' warns about the dangers of over-ambition

- *Frankenstein* is the story of a young <u>scientist</u>, Victor Frankenstein, who creates a living <u>monster</u> out of dead bodies. This results in the <u>deaths</u> of most of his friends and family, and eventually of Frankenstein himself.

- It's regarded as one of the <u>most influential</u> novels in English literature, and it's often considered to be the <u>first science fiction</u> story.

Frankenstein has two strong messages:

- <u>Ambition</u> has the power to be <u>dangerous</u>, particularly if it's selfishly or recklessly pursued, and it can lead to <u>death</u> and <u>destruction</u>.

- Certain <u>knowledge</u> is forbidden — and mankind <u>shouldn't</u> meddle with it as the consequences could be terrible.

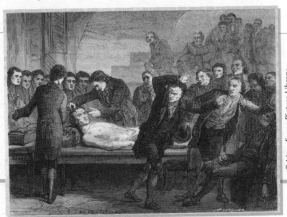

© Mary Evans Picture Library

An engraving of Andrew Ure's 1818 experiment to reanimate the corpse of a dead criminal.

Mary Shelley had a literary background

1) Mary Shelley was the <u>child</u> of two famous <u>writers</u> — Mary Wollstonecraft, an early <u>feminist</u>, and William Godwin, a controversial <u>political writer</u>. Many of her parents' <u>friends</u> were also writers.

2) Shelley <u>married</u> the <u>'Romantic' poet</u> Percy Bysshe Shelley. They <u>travelled</u> through Europe together, and many of the <u>locations</u> they visited are <u>mentioned</u> in *Frankenstein*.

1797	<u>Born</u> on 30th August, in <u>London</u>. Her mother <u>dies</u> just days later from complications.
1812-14	Goes to stay in <u>Scotland</u> with friends. The beautiful <u>scenery</u> inspires her to begin writing.
1814	<u>Elopes</u> to Switzerland with the married <u>poet</u> Percy Bysshe Shelley.
1815	Gives birth to a <u>child</u>, who <u>dies</u> shortly after.
1816	Writes a <u>short story</u> during a stay at <u>Lake Geneva</u>, which would later be <u>adapted</u> into 'Frankenstein'.
	<u>Marries</u> Percy after his first wife <u>drowns</u>.
1818	'Frankenstein' is published.
1822	Percy <u>dies</u> in a boating accident.
1831	<u>Revised edition</u> of 'Frankenstein' published.
1851	<u>Dies</u>, aged 53.

© Mary Evans/Epic/Tallandier

Background Information

'Frankenstein' is set in Europe

Here's a <u>map</u> of the main locations in the novel:

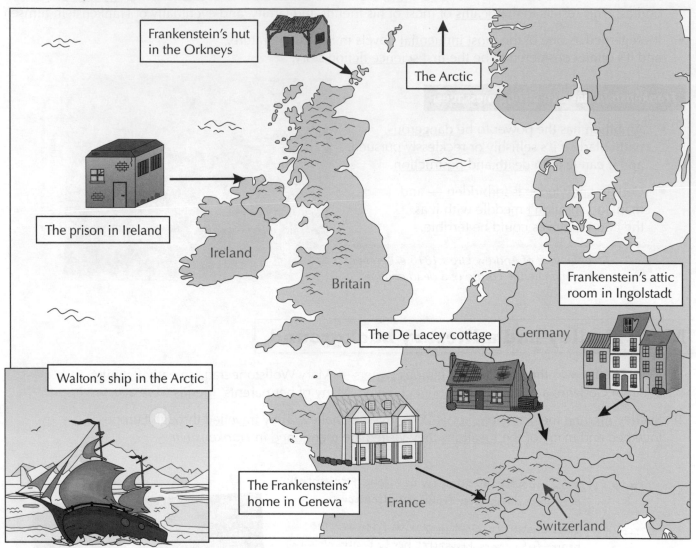

Frankenstein's hut in the Orkneys

The Arctic

The prison in Ireland

Ireland

Britain

Frankenstein's attic room in Ingolstadt

The De Lacey cottage

Germany

Walton's ship in the Arctic

The Frankensteins' home in Geneva

France

Switzerland

Mary Shelley wrote 'Frankenstein' in Geneva

1) When Mary Shelley started writing *Frankenstein* in 1816, she and Percy Bysshe Shelley were staying with Lord Byron (a 'Romantic' poet) at his villa on the shores of <u>Lake Geneva</u>, in Switzerland.

2) During their stay, <u>bad weather</u> forced Mary and her companions to spend a lot of time indoors. To pass the time, they read <u>ghost stories</u>. They then challenged each other to <u>write</u> one, but Mary struggled to think of a good plot.

3) After a discussion about science, Mary had a <u>dream</u> in which she saw a "<u>pale student</u> of <u>unhallowed arts</u> kneeling beside the <u>thing</u> he had put together". This dream inspired her to write her story.

4) Mary expanded the story into a <u>novel</u>, *Frankenstein*, which was <u>published</u> in 1818. After lots of <u>editing</u>, a <u>second</u> version was published in 1831.

This text guide uses the 1831 edition of the novel.

Introduction

Who's Who in 'Frankenstein'

Victor Frankenstein...

...is an ambitious young scientist who becomes obsessed with bringing inanimate matter to life.

The Monster...

...is Frankenstein's creation. He's hideously ugly, and becomes bitter and evil after being rejected by society.

Robert Walton...

...is an ambitious explorer who's travelling to the North Pole. He's determined to succeed, but he's also lonely.

Henry Clerval...

...is Frankenstein's best friend. He's cheerful, loyal and adventurous, with a passion for learning.

Elizabeth Lavenza...

...is the Frankenstein family's adopted child, and Victor's friend and fiancée. She's beautiful, kind and caring.

Alphonse Frankenstein...

...is Frankenstein's father, and a distinguished public figure in Geneva. He adores his wife and family.

William Frankenstein...

...is the youngest child of the Frankenstein family. He's an attractive and cheerful child who's well-loved.

Justine Moritz...

...is the Frankensteins' servant. She's loyal and kind, and she's particularly attached to William.

De Lacey...

...is a kind, blind old man who's been exiled from his home in France. He's looked after by his son and daughter.

'Frankenstein' — Plot Summary

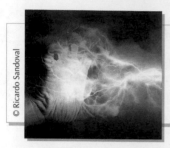

'Frankenstein'... what happens when?

Frankenstein has got loads of drama for you to get your teeth into. You'll need to learn exactly when all the juicy stuff happens, so that in the exam you'll be ready to write a top-notch answer. Here's a handy plot summary to get you started...

Letters 1 to 4 — Robert Walton rescues Victor Frankenstein

- The novel opens with a series of <u>letters</u>, written from Robert Walton to his <u>sister</u> in England. Walton is trying to fulfil a lifelong <u>dream</u> of sailing to the <u>North Pole</u>.

- His crew spot a <u>sledge</u> in the <u>icy</u> surroundings, ridden by a <u>huge man</u>. The next day, they see <u>another</u> sledge, and pull its <u>sickly</u> occupant, Victor Frankenstein, aboard.

- Walton tells Frankenstein about his <u>passionate ambition</u> to reach the pole. Frankenstein decides to tell Walton his <u>own story</u>, in order to <u>warn</u> him about the dangers of ambition.

Chapters 1 to 10 — Frankenstein makes a monster

- Frankenstein has a <u>happy childhood</u> — he's loved by his <u>parents</u>, and enjoys the companionship of his adoptive <u>sister</u>, Elizabeth, and his <u>best friend</u>, Henry Clerval. From a young age, Frankenstein is also passionate about <u>science</u>.

- When he's seventeen, Frankenstein goes to <u>university</u> in Ingolstadt. Whilst at university, he becomes <u>obsessed</u> with creating <u>life</u> from dead matter.

- Frankenstein <u>succeeds</u> in creating a living man out of corpses — but the being is horrifically <u>ugly</u>, and Frankenstein <u>flees</u> in terror. The monster <u>disappears</u>.

- The <u>shock</u> of his creation makes Frankenstein <u>ill</u>. Eventually he <u>recovers</u>, only to learn that his youngest <u>brother</u>, William, has been <u>murdered</u>.

- Frankenstein returns to <u>Geneva</u>, where his family live. He sees the <u>monster</u> near where William was <u>murdered</u> and guesses that he's responsible for William's death.

- The Frankensteins' <u>servant</u>, Justine Moritz, has been <u>arrested</u> for murdering William. Elizabeth tries to <u>defend</u> her, but she's found <u>guilty</u> and <u>executed</u>.

- Frankenstein feels <u>guilty</u> about William and Justine's deaths. He takes a <u>trip</u> to the <u>Alps</u> to find comfort in its beautiful scenery. At the top of a <u>mountain</u> the <u>monster</u> appears, and he persuades Frankenstein to <u>listen</u> to his <u>story</u>.

Chapters 11 to 16 — The monster tells his story

- The <u>monster</u> describes how he was <u>attacked</u> by everyone who met him. He took shelter in a hovel, and learned to <u>speak</u> by <u>eavesdropping</u> on the De Lacey family.

- Eventually the monster <u>approached</u> them, hoping to be taken into their <u>family</u>, but they <u>rejected</u> him and <u>fled</u>. In <u>anger</u>, the monster <u>burned</u> their house down.

- The monster went to Geneva to find Frankenstein. On his way there, he <u>saved</u> a girl from drowning, but her male companion <u>shot</u> the monster in fear.

- In Geneva, the monster met Frankenstein's <u>brother</u>, William. The monster tried to make <u>friends</u> with him, but after finding out that he was <u>related</u> to Frankenstein, he <u>killed</u> him. He then found Justine <u>asleep</u> in a barn, and slipped William's <u>locket</u> into the folds of her dress, <u>framing</u> her.

- The monster <u>finishes</u> his story, and asks Frankenstein to <u>create</u> him a female <u>companion</u>.

Chapters 17 to 24 — Things go from bad to worse

- The monster says he'll leave humanity <u>alone</u> if Frankenstein creates a <u>companion</u> for him, so Frankenstein agrees to build a <u>female</u> monster.

- Frankenstein <u>travels</u> through <u>Britain</u> with Clerval, then goes alone to the <u>Orkney Islands</u> and begins to <u>work</u>. However, he has a change of heart and <u>destroys</u> his creation. The monster appears and promises <u>revenge</u>.

- Frankenstein sails out to <u>sea</u> to <u>dispose</u> of his work, but he's swept by a <u>storm</u> to the <u>Irish</u> coast, where he's immediately <u>arrested</u> for <u>murder</u>. The victim is Henry Clerval, presumably killed by the <u>monster</u>. The <u>shock</u> of Henry's death makes Frankenstein very <u>ill</u>.

- Frankenstein <u>recovers</u> and is found <u>innocent</u>. His father takes him back to Geneva, and Frankenstein and Elizabeth <u>marry</u>.

- On their wedding night, the monster <u>kills</u> Elizabeth. Frankenstein is <u>devastated</u>, and Alphonse <u>dies</u> of <u>heartbreak</u>.

- Alone, Frankenstein <u>pursues</u> the monster to the Arctic, but fails to <u>capture</u> him.

The <u>narrative</u> returns to Walton, who describes Frankenstein's <u>death</u>. Walton then finds the monster <u>mourning</u> over Frankenstein's body. The monster says that he'll commit <u>suicide</u> now that his <u>creator</u> is <u>dead</u>, and leaves.

Not exactly a happy ending...

Three narratives, multiple deaths and a whole lot of misery later, you've reached the end of the plot. There's a cartoon in the back of this book if you want something less wordy to help you remember everything — or you can make yourself a cup of tea and move on to the next section. World's your oyster, really.

Shelley and Contemporary Science

When *Frankenstein* was published, some people were shocked that a young woman had invented such a terrifying story. But the idea of using a "spark" to bring a dead body to life wasn't actually that nuts at the time.

Shelley was inspired by contemporary science

1) Shelley was writing at a time of great <u>scientific debate</u> about the <u>origins of life</u>. Some scientists believed that studying <u>electricity</u> might reveal what gives life to people and animals.

2) In 1780, <u>Luigi Galvani</u> found that connecting two different metals to a <u>dead frog</u> would generate an electric current and move the frog's <u>muscles</u>. Galvani decided there was a type of '<u>animal electricity</u>' (later called '<u>galvanism</u>') within living things, responsible for muscle movement.

3) In 1803, Giovanni Aldini (Galvani's nephew) conducted a similar experiment on the body of a <u>dead criminal</u>. People reported seeing the jaw <u>quiver</u> and an <u>eye</u> open.

Experiments like this led to '<u>body-snatching</u>', where criminals illegally dug up corpses and sold them to medical schools. This was seen as <u>blasphemous</u> (disrespectful to God) and caused <u>outrage</u>.

Shelley was aware of these experiments when she wrote *Frankenstein*. In her <u>introduction</u> to the 1831 edition of the novel, she wrote about a conversation she listened to between Percy Bysshe Shelley and Lord Byron where they discussed whether "a <u>corpse</u> would be <u>reanimated</u>" and if "a creature might be <u>manufactured</u>... and endued with <u>vital warmth</u>."

4) Inspired by scientists like Galvani and Aldini, Shelley implies that Frankenstein uses electricity to <u>animate</u> the monster — he infuses a "<u>spark of being</u>" into a "<u>lifeless thing</u>".

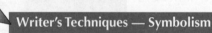

Writer's Techniques — Symbolism

<u>Sparks</u> and <u>lightning</u> are symbols for <u>knowledge</u> in the novel, but they're also associated with <u>danger</u>: a tree near Frankenstein's home is "utterly destroyed" by lightning.

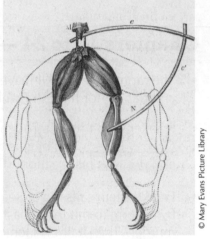
A sketch of Galvani's experiment

Explorers were travelling to the Arctic in the early 1800s

1) When Shelley wrote *Frankenstein* there was great interest in <u>polar exploration</u>. The British government was preparing two Arctic expeditions, ready to depart in <u>1818</u>.

2) Since the 1500s, Britain had been trying to find a <u>shorter passage</u> to India and China through the <u>Arctic</u> seas. This would provide a more efficient <u>trading</u> route to these countries.

3) Expeditions to find this passage were very <u>dangerous</u>, and many explorers had <u>failed</u>. However, explorers knew that if they succeeded, they would return to Britain as <u>heroes</u>.

Character — Walton

Like the real-life explorers of his day, <u>Walton</u> wants to find a "<u>passage</u>" through the Arctic. He thinks this will bring an "<u>inestimable benefit</u>" to mankind, and will bring him personal "<u>glory</u>". He's willing to risk <u>danger</u> and even death to succeed.

KEY QUOTE

"I might infuse a spark of being into the lifeless thing"

Shelley didn't pluck the idea for *Frankenstein* out of thin air. Percy and Byron's chat prompted her to have a vivid dream about a student bringing a creature to life, which gave her the idea for the novel. Handy, eh?

Rousseau and the 'Romantics'

So, Mary Shelley absorbed some of the biggest philosophical ideas of her time and used them to write a work of literary genius, which is still read and studied over two hundred years later. Not bad for a nineteen year old.

Rousseau wrote about mankind's natural innocence

1) Jean-Jacques Rousseau was an influential 18th century philosopher who was born in Geneva. Shelley had read his work, and his ideas had a big influence on *Frankenstein*.

2) Rousseau argued that mankind would be happier in a natural state where organised society doesn't exist and everyone is free and equal. He believed that society corrupts humans because it creates inequality and jealousy.

There's more on society and prejudice on p.40-41.

Character — The Monster

Early in his life, the monster is a 'natural' being, separate from organised society. He says he was "benevolent and good" at this time. Later, when he learns about society, he's changed for the worse and becomes a "fiend".

3) Rousseau also argued that someone abandoned at birth, with no companionship or instruction, would be distorted by society's prejudices until they became "the most disfigured of all". In the novel, the monster is abandoned at 'birth' by Frankenstein, and is then driven to misery and murder by prejudice in society.

- Rousseau's ideas about society, freedom and equality influenced the leaders of the French Revolution, which began in 1789. The revolutionaries hated the inequality they saw in society, so they overthrew the monarchy and killed the king.

- Many people hoped that the Revolution would lead to a fairer society, but it descended into brutal violence and led to huge wars in Europe.

- *Frankenstein* was written in the aftermath of these wars. Some people see the novel as a warning about how good intentions (such as Frankenstein's desire to "banish disease") can lead to violence and destruction.

The 'Romantic' movement influenced Shelley

1) The 'Romantic' movement had a major impact on art and literature in the late 1700s and early 1800s. Mary Shelley's husband, Percy Bysshe Shelley, was a famous 'Romantic' poet.

2) The 'Romantics' tried to capture intense emotions and experiences in their work, especially those associated with nature. For the 'Romantics', nature is a powerful force that can inspire and restore people.

3) There are many 'Romantic' settings in the novel. For example, after William and Justine's deaths, Frankenstein visits the Alps, where he feels a "tingling long-lost sense of pleasure" and receives "the greatest consolation".

There's more on the novel's settings on page 50.

Character — Clerval

Nature has a particularly powerful effect on Clerval. As he travels down the river Rhine, he feels "a happiness seldom tasted by man".

A 'Romantic' painting.

You can make links to the ideas of Shelley's time...

Writing about Rousseau or the 'Romantics' is a sure-fire way to impress the examiner. Just name-dropping isn't enough, though — you'll need to say how their ideas are reflected in the text to get the marks.

'Paradise Lost' and 'Prometheus'

Shelley references many works of literature in *Frankenstein*, but there are a couple that you'll really need to know about in order to understand the novel. I've written you a page about them. You can thank me later.

'Paradise Lost' is a key influence on the story

Making links to another text to suggest ideas to the reader is known as 'intertextuality'.

1) *Paradise Lost* is a poem by <u>John Milton</u> based on the book of <u>Genesis</u> from the Bible.

2) Genesis tells the story of God's creation of the Earth and of <u>Adam and Eve</u>. God forbids Adam and Eve from eating the fruit from the <u>tree of knowledge</u>, but Satan persuades them to disobey God, and they're <u>exiled</u> from the Garden of Eden.

Theme — Knowledge

Like Adam and Eve, Frankenstein meddles with <u>forbidden knowledge</u> and suffers misery and isolation as a result.

3) In Milton's poem, <u>Satan</u> has been thrown out of Heaven for rebelling against God, so he decides to take <u>revenge</u> by corrupting Adam and Eve. Unlike in the Bible, Milton's poem shows both Satan and Adam <u>questioning</u> God's actions.

© Mary Evans Picture Library

An illustration of Satan from 'Paradise Lost'.

On the <u>title page</u> of the first edition of *Frankenstein* there are three of Adam's lines from *Paradise Lost*, in which he <u>questions God</u> for creating him:

> Did I request thee, Maker, from my clay
> To mould Me man? Did I solicit thee
> From darkness to promote me?

This suggests that the novel should be read with *Paradise Lost* <u>in mind</u>. Like Adam, the <u>monster</u> questions his creator for making him, since his life is so miserable.

4) There are many <u>references</u> to the poem in *Frankenstein*. For example:

- After he reads *Paradise Lost*, the <u>monster</u> compares himself to <u>Satan</u>, because they're both <u>outcasts</u>. However, the monster is also upset that even Satan had "companions", whilst he is "<u>solitary</u>".

- The monster also compares himself to <u>Adam</u>. He <u>complains</u> that Adam was "guarded by the especial care of his Creator", whilst he's been "<u>abandoned</u>" by Frankenstein.

- The monster thinks that his relationship with <u>Frankenstein</u> should be like <u>Adam</u> and <u>God's</u> — "I am thy creature; I ought to be thy Adam".

The novel's alternative title is 'The Modern Prometheus'

1) Prometheus is a character in Greek and Roman <u>mythology</u>. There are <u>two versions</u> of the Prometheus myth:

In the Greek myth, mankind is <u>forbidden</u> by the gods to have <u>fire</u>, but Prometheus <u>steals</u> it for mankind and <u>teaches</u> them how to use it.

The Romans added to the myth the idea that Prometheus <u>created man</u> using clay and water.

2) Prometheus is <u>eternally punished</u> by the god Zeus (Jupiter, in Roman mythology) for stealing fire.

3) Frankenstein is a 'modern Prometheus' because he also <u>creates a man</u> and wants to benefit mankind with <u>forbidden knowledge</u>. Like Prometheus, Frankenstein's actions cause him <u>pain</u> and <u>misery</u>.

4) Prometheus has often been portrayed as a rebellious <u>hero</u>, challenging the gods and the <u>laws of creation</u>, and Frankenstein presents himself in a <u>similar</u> way.

KEY QUOTE

"I ought to be thy Adam; but I am rather the fallen angel"

Paradise Lost references are <u>everywhere</u> in this novel — characters are constantly chatting about devils and creators and so on. Make sure you know enough to spot these fiendish little phrases when they pop up.

Section One — Background and Context

Practice Questions

Shelley packed a whole host of contemporary ideas into 'Frankenstein' — it's time to see if you can unpack them. Don't panic — all the answers can be found in this section. You only need to write a few words or a sentence for the quick questions, and a couple of lines or a paragraph for the in-depth ones.

Quick Questions

1) What did Luigi Galvani use to move the muscles of a dead frog in 1780?

2) Who continued Galvani's work with an experiment on a dead criminal in 1803?

3) Give one reason why explorers wanted to find a passage through the Arctic seas.

4) According to Jean-Jacques Rousseau, in what way does society corrupt humans?

5) Which revolution did Jean-Jacques Rousseau's ideas inspire the leaders of?

6) Write down two things that the 'Romantics' tried to capture in their work.

7) a) Who wrote *Paradise Lost*?
   b) Which book of the Bible is it based on?
   c) Where in the first edition of *Frankenstein* can you find three of Adam's lines from this poem?

8) What did the Romans add to the Greek myth about Prometheus?

In-depth Questions

1) To what extent are Shelley's presentations of Frankenstein and Walton influenced by the scientists and explorers of her time?

2) Explain how Shelley's presentation of the monster can be linked to the ideas of Jean-Jacques Rousseau.

3) "*Frankenstein* is strongly influenced by the 'Romantic' movement."
   Give an example from the text to support this statement and explain why you've chosen it.

4) Explain at least one similarity between each of the following pairs of characters from *Frankenstein* and *Paradise Lost*:
   a) Frankenstein and God
   b) The monster and Adam
   c) The monster and Satan

5) Briefly explain why Victor Frankenstein can be seen as 'The Modern Prometheus'.

Analysis of Walton's Letters

It's time for some detailed analysis of the novel, but make sure you've read *Frankenstein* before you press on.

'Frankenstein' starts with Walton's point of view

1) *Frankenstein* begins with a series of <u>letters</u>, written by an explorer, Robert Walton, to his sister.

2) In the letters, Walton explains his <u>ambition</u> to go to the North Pole and <u>discover</u> its secrets, so that he might bring "inestimable benefit... on all mankind". He also reveals his loneliness and desire for a <u>companion</u>.

3) Walton travels to the Arctic, and in this "<u>wild</u> and mysterious" wasteland a <u>man</u> (Victor Frankenstein) is pulled aboard Walton's ship. This <u>unexpected event</u> makes the reader <u>curious</u> about why the man is there.

4) Shelley introduces Frankenstein when he's in the <u>middle</u> of a <u>chase</u>. By introducing him in this way, Shelley creates <u>excitement</u> and <u>tension</u>.

> **Writer's Techniques — Form**
>
> *Frankenstein* is an <u>epistolary</u> novel — it uses <u>letters</u> to tell a story. See p.46 for more about this.

Walton admires Frankenstein

1) Walton is quick to <u>admire</u> Frankenstein — he sees him as the <u>companion</u> that he's been hoping for. He says Frankenstein is "gentle" and "wise", and that he loves him "as a <u>brother</u>".

2) Walton sees Frankenstein as a <u>kindred spirit</u>, and he tells him about his ambitious quest for <u>knowledge</u>. However, Frankenstein sees his own <u>flaws</u> in Walton and reacts with <u>horror</u>. He asks Walton if he shares his "<u>madness</u>" and whether he's "drunk also of the intoxicating draught" of <u>ambition</u>.

3) Frankenstein tells Walton his <u>story</u> in the hope that it'll "direct" him in his <u>dangerous</u> search for <u>knowledge</u>.

© Everett Collection/REX

Walton's narrative introduces key themes

The <u>events</u> in Walton's <u>narrative</u> introduce some <u>themes</u> which become <u>important</u> later in the novel:

- The dangers of <u>ambition</u>, and of the reckless pursuit of <u>knowledge</u>, are themes introduced in Walton's narrative. Frankenstein hopes that his story will <u>warn</u> Walton about these <u>dangers</u>.

- <u>Isolation</u> is also a theme that's introduced in Walton's <u>letters</u>. Walton is lonely, and <u>needs</u> a <u>companion</u> to "sympathise" with him and to "repair" his "faults", while Frankenstein claims that humans are only "<u>half</u> made up" without a friend. Later in the novel, the <u>monster's isolation</u> contributes to his <u>misery</u>.

  For more about these themes, see Section Four.

- Walton's letters show the importance of <u>family</u>, as he expresses "<u>gratitude</u>" for his sister's "love and kindness". <u>Family love</u>, or a lack of it, is also an <u>important</u> theme in both Frankenstein's and the monster's narratives in the novel.

Talk about the novel's structure in your exam...

Shelley's structure is complicated — you get lots of different narratives and styles of writing, including the <u>epistolary form</u> (letters). You'll get marks for analysing form and structure, so check out p.46-47 for more.

Analysis of Chapters 1 and 2

Frankenstein's narrative starts at the very beginning of his life. We get to learn all about his childhood...

Frankenstein had a very happy childhood

1) Frankenstein's <u>family</u> was "<u>distinguished</u>", and his <u>father</u>, Alphonse, was <u>respected</u> for his "integrity".

2) Alphonse is described as being "like a <u>protecting</u> spirit" to Frankenstein's <u>mother</u>, Caroline. Their <u>marriage</u> is one of "devoted <u>affection</u>".

3) Frankenstein's <u>earliest memories</u> are of his mother's "tender caresses" and his father's "benevolent" smile, and he says that "No human being could have passed a <u>happier</u> childhood".

> ### Theme — Family
> Frankenstein's family <u>love</u> him with "<u>inexhaustible</u> stores of affection". This <u>contrasts</u> with the way Frankenstein later treats the <u>monster</u>.

Elizabeth and Clerval are ideal companions

1) Elizabeth Lavenza was adopted by Frankenstein's parents at a young age. Shelley emphasises her angelic nature — she's "sweet", and "fairer" than a "<u>cherub</u>". She has a <u>strong bond</u> with Frankenstein.

2) Henry Clerval is Frankenstein's best friend and he's presented as a <u>good person</u>, full of "kindness and tenderness". He's <u>ambitious</u> like Frankenstein and Walton, but <u>unlike</u> them his ambition never gets out of <u>control</u>.

3) Frankenstein enjoys remembering his former <u>happiness</u>, before the "tale of misery" that followed. Shelley reminds the reader that the <u>happiness</u> of Frankenstein's childhood won't <u>last</u>, and that <u>tragedy</u> will follow.

© ITV/REX

> ### Character — Elizabeth
> Elizabeth's <u>influence</u> ensures that "doing <u>good</u>" is Clerval's <u>priority</u> in life, and she <u>improves</u> Frankenstein's "<u>sullen</u>" temperament. However, she can't <u>stop</u> Frankenstein destructively pursuing his <u>ambition</u>.

Frankenstein has a passion for knowledge

1) Frankenstein describes his <u>early love</u> of <u>natural philosophers</u> (Agrippa, Magnus and Paracelsus). His <u>enthusiasm</u> for the "elixir of <u>life</u>" and raising "ghosts or <u>devils</u>" hints at what he'll later <u>create</u>.

2) After meeting a <u>scientist</u> who teaches him about <u>galvanism</u> (see p.6), Frankenstein starts to see the work of the old philosophers as "<u>despicable</u>" and a "deformed and abortive creation". This hints at the way he'll later see the <u>monster</u> — the creation they <u>inspire</u>.

3) Frankenstein turns to studying <u>maths</u> instead, which he describes as the "last effort" of a "guardian angel" to turn him onto the <u>right path</u>. However, Frankenstein claims that <u>destiny</u> is "too potent", and that he was <u>doomed</u> to the "<u>destruction</u>" that followed.

> ### Character — Frankenstein
> Frankenstein often refers to the events of the novel as being driven by <u>fate</u>. He could be doing this to avoid taking <u>responsibility</u> for his <u>actions</u>.

KEY QUOTE

"No human being could have passed a happier childhood"

The first few chapters are dedicated to explaining just how perfect Frankenstein's family and friends were. Just to make it that little bit more painful when they all get killed off later. Thanks, Mary, thanks a lot.

Analysis of Chapters 3 to 5

It's all downhill from here... Frankenstein explains how studying at university gave him the knowledge he needed to create new life. These days, a lot of people just learn how to make beans on toast...

Frankenstein is inspired at university

1) After Frankenstein's mother <u>dies</u>, he goes to <u>university</u> in Ingolstadt. Professor Waldman <u>inspires</u> him — he claims modern scientists are <u>god-like</u>, they "ascend into the <u>heavens</u>" with "almost <u>unlimited</u> powers".

2) Waldman's words make Frankenstein think he can "<u>pioneer</u> a new way" and "explore unknown <u>powers</u>". Shelley's language emphasises the <u>grandeur</u> of Frankenstein's ambitions, which makes his eventual <u>downfall</u> seem more <u>tragic</u>.

Writer's Techniques

Frankenstein talks about <u>science</u> as if he's an <u>explorer</u> going on an <u>expedition</u>. His <u>language</u> is similar to Walton's, which emphasises the parallels between the two characters (see p.28).

3) Frankenstein continues to suggest that <u>fate</u> influences his actions. He claims "the <u>Angel of Destruction</u>" led him to meet Waldman, and says that this was the day that "<u>decided</u>" his "<u>destiny</u>".

Frankenstein learns how to bring inanimate matter to life

1) Frankenstein finds a way to make a <u>living being</u> from <u>dead bodies</u>. He thinks his work will <u>benefit</u> humanity, saying that he can "pour a torrent of light" into the "dark world".

Theme — Creation

According to the <u>Bible</u>, the <u>first</u> act of God in <u>creating</u> the Earth was to separate the <u>light</u> from the <u>darkness</u>. Frankenstein's words link him to <u>God</u> and creation of <u>life</u>.

© Moviestore Collection/REX

2) However, Frankenstein also has selfish motivations — he's <u>excited</u> that his creations would "<u>owe</u> their being" to him.

3) Frankenstein <u>obsessively</u> dedicates himself to his task, <u>ignoring</u> his friends and family, and the "charms of nature". Shelley presents his work as <u>disturbing</u> and <u>unclean</u> — Frankenstein spends his time in his "workshop of <u>filthy</u> creation", and he says he would often "turn with <u>loathing</u>" from his work.

Frankenstein gives life to his creation

KEY EVENT

1) When Frankenstein brings the monster to life, his reaction suggests it's <u>repulsive</u> — it makes him feel a "breathless <u>horror</u> and disgust".

2) Frankenstein <u>flees</u> before the monster can <u>do</u> anything. This is the first time the monster suffers <u>prejudice</u>.

Writer's Techniques

After creating the monster, Frankenstein has a <u>dream</u> where Elizabeth transforms into the "<u>corpse</u>" of his dead mother. This <u>foreshadows</u> Elizabeth's death. (Foreshadowing is when a writer gives the reader clues about what will happen later in the story, for more see p.47.)

3) Henry Clerval arrives in Ingolstadt soon <u>after</u> the monster <u>awakens</u>. This creates a more cheerful <u>tone</u> in the narrative, and contrasts with Frankenstein's <u>horror</u> at what he's done.

4) Frankenstein becomes <u>hysterical</u> and falls <u>ill</u>. Clerval <u>nurses</u> him through the <u>sickness</u> until he's well again.

EXAM TIP

Mention the early signs of Frankenstein's obsession...

There are loads of signs that Frankenstein's obsession with science is going to be a problem. Having a future-Frankenstein narrate his past actions means that he can tell us exactly where he went wrong.

Analysis of Chapters 6 to 8

Victor goes home, where things are getting intense. You could say he arrives *Justine* time for the excitement...

Frankenstein recovers — but his happiness is short-lived

KEY EVENT

1) Elizabeth sends a <u>letter</u> with news of Frankenstein's brothers and descriptions of their <u>happy home life</u>. The cheerful letter provides another <u>contrast</u> to the <u>disturbing</u> nature of Frankenstein's work in Ingolstadt.

Writer's Techniques

Shelley uses the <u>letters</u> from Geneva to <u>inform</u> the reader about events that have happened <u>outside</u> of Ingolstadt.

2) Frankenstein gives up science and studies <u>languages</u>. He's able to find <u>joy</u> in life again as he enjoys Clerval's <u>companionship</u>, and <u>nature</u> fills him with "<u>ecstasy</u>".

Theme — Revenge

Alphonse warns Frankenstein against "thoughts of <u>vengeance</u>". His reaction to William's murder <u>contrasts</u> with the way that both Frankenstein and the monster <u>react</u> to tragedies.

3) However, Frankenstein's brief happiness is <u>shattered</u> when another letter, from his <u>father</u>, tells him that his <u>brother</u>, William, has been <u>murdered</u>.

4) Frankenstein sets off for <u>home</u>. He reminds the reader again that he "was <u>destined</u> to become the most <u>wretched</u> of human beings" which suggests that even <u>worse</u> events are yet to come.

The monster appears during a violent storm

1) Frankenstein <u>returns</u> to Geneva, but he arrives <u>after</u> the city gates have <u>closed</u> for the night, so he decides to visit the <u>scene</u> of William's <u>murder</u>.

2) During a storm, a <u>lightning</u> flash reveals the "<u>hideous</u>" figure of the monster. The <u>stormy weather</u> makes the event seem more <u>dramatic</u> and <u>frightening</u>.

3) Frankenstein thinks the monster killed William. He calls him "filthy demon" and "animal", emphasising his <u>inhuman</u> appearance. Frankenstein's language <u>encourages</u> the reader to <u>share</u> his <u>loathing</u> of the monster.

© Moviestore Collection/REX

Justine is wrongly convicted of William's murder

1) Frankenstein learns that Justine, a <u>servant</u> in Frankenstein's family, has been accused of William's <u>murder</u>. Frankenstein is sure that she's <u>innocent</u>, but he has no <u>evidence</u> that the monster killed William, and he doesn't think anyone would <u>believe</u> him if he spoke out.

2) Elizabeth also believes that Justine is <u>innocent</u>. She speaks passionately to the court, trying to <u>persuade</u> the judges of Justine's innocence, but it isn't enough to prevent Justine's <u>conviction</u> and <u>execution</u>.

3) Frankenstein suffers "bitter agony" over Justine's death. He feels <u>guilty</u> about it, and he describes William and Justine as his "first... <u>victims</u>" — which hints that there will be more victims to come.

Theme — Society

Justine's trial and execution suggest that there are <u>flaws</u> in society's institutions — despite what Alphonse thinks, it seems that people <u>can't</u> "rely on the justice" of the law (see p.40 for more on society).

KEY QUOTE

"Nothing in human shape could have destroyed that fair child"

Ding dong, irony alert. Frankenstein sees William as so perfect that only something truly beastly could've killed him — but in creating the monster, he's kind of responsible for his death. Who's the real monster?

Analysis of Chapters 9 and 10

This is a fairly climactic part of the novel — after hearing Frankenstein's side of the story, the reader finally gets to get up close and personal with the monster. As it turns out, he's surprisingly chatty...

Frankenstein suffers despair and remorse

1) Frankenstein can't <u>sleep</u> and wanders "like an evil spirit". <u>Grief</u> makes him <u>isolate</u> himself from his <u>family</u>, and seek "deep, dark, deathlike solitude".

2) He feels <u>fury</u> and <u>hatred</u>, and his desire for <u>revenge</u> is uncontrollable — it "burst all bounds of moderation". Frankenstein's <u>intense</u>, <u>violent</u> style of <u>language</u> is <u>similar</u> to that of the monster later on.

3) Frankenstein hopes that the "magnificence" of <u>nature</u> will help him <u>forget</u> his "sorrows", so he <u>rides</u> to the valley of Chamounix.

> **Writer's Techniques — Setting**
>
> The <u>landscape</u> that Frankenstein visits is <u>beautiful</u> but <u>unfriendly</u>, with "<u>immense</u> mountains" and "<u>shattered</u> pines". This remote setting <u>emphasises</u> the <u>isolation</u> that he's <u>forcing</u> himself into.

Frankenstein and the monster finally meet

KEY EVENT

1) Frankenstein calls to "Wandering spirits" to either let him be <u>happy</u>, or take him "<u>away</u> from the joys of life". A <u>wandering</u> <u>figure</u> does appear, but it's not a spirit — it's the monster.

2) Frankenstein reacts with "<u>rage</u>", and prepares to <u>attack</u> the monster. However, Frankenstein mentions that the monster's appearance "bespoke bitter <u>anguish</u>", which suggests that the monster has suffered his own personal tragedies.

3) The monster reveals that he's "<u>miserable</u> beyond all living things", making the reader curious about the monster's life so far. It also makes the reader begin to <u>question</u> Frankenstein's <u>reaction</u> to him.

© JONES Pete/ArenaPAL

The monster reasons with Frankenstein

1) Until now, neither the reader nor Frankenstein has heard the monster speak, but we discover that he's able to <u>speak eloquently</u>. He reminds Frankenstein of his <u>responsibilities</u> to him as his maker — "Do your <u>duty</u> towards me".

2) The monster questions Frankenstein's desire to kill him, asking "How dare you <u>sport</u> thus with life?" The monster's <u>judgement</u> also makes the reader question Frankenstein's <u>behaviour</u>.

3) The monster warns Frankenstein that if he doesn't help him, he'll "glut the maw of <u>death</u>" (feed the mouth of death) with the "<u>blood</u>" of his "<u>remaining</u> friends". This threat emphasises that the monster can be <u>violent</u>, and implies that he's <u>responsible</u> for William's <u>death</u>.

> **Background and Context**
>
> The monster references Genesis and *Paradise Lost* (see p.8) when he compares Frankenstein to <u>God</u> and himself to <u>Adam</u> — "I ought to be thy Adam". However, he says that <u>now</u> he's more like "the fallen angel", <u>Satan</u>.

> **Character — The Monster**
>
> The monster <u>covers</u> Frankenstein's <u>eyes</u>, saying that he's <u>relieving</u> Frankenstein from seeing his <u>ugliness</u>. He knows that his appearance <u>upsets</u> Frankenstein, and tries to <u>persuade</u> him with his words instead.

> **KEY QUOTE**
>
> ### *"All men hate the wretched; how, then, must I be hated"*
>
> The monster is a persuasive speaker — he appeals to Frankenstein's compassion, and successfully convinces him to listen to his story. It's then up to the reader to make a judgement on whether or not he's in the right.

Analysis of Chapters 11 and 12

Now the monster gets to tell the depressing tale of his lonely beginnings in life.

The monster starts to tell his story

1) The <u>narrative voice changes</u>, and the monster tells his <u>story</u>, which:

   - Fills in the <u>gaps</u> of his <u>early life</u> that Frankenstein doesn't <u>know</u> about.
   - Allows the reader to see the monster's <u>perspective</u>, and <u>contrast</u> it with Frankenstein's.
   - Gives the reader an <u>insight</u> into the monster's <u>emotions</u>, making him more <u>sympathetic</u>.

2) The monster's early <u>memories</u> are <u>confused</u> impressions of <u>light</u> and <u>temperature</u>. He later suffers from <u>fatigue</u>, <u>hunger</u> and <u>pain</u>. Shelley uses the monster's narrative to emphasise his <u>vulnerability</u> — he says that he was "frightened" and "helpless", which helps the reader to <u>pity</u> him.

3) The monster <u>learns</u> quickly, finding a cloak to <u>cover</u> himself and using a <u>fire</u> to cook, which shows his <u>intelligence</u> and <u>instinct to survive</u>. He even begins to appreciate <u>nature</u>, and tries to <u>imitate</u> birdsong.

Every human the monster meets reacts with horror

1) The monster is "<u>enchanted</u>" by a shepherd's hut, and a village seems "<u>miraculous</u>" to him. His <u>wonder</u> at such everyday things emphasises his <u>innocence</u>.

2) However, he's <u>attacked</u> by the people who live in the <u>village</u>. Their <u>cruel behaviour</u> contrasts with the monster's <u>innocent</u> appreciation of the village, so their treatment of him feels <u>shocking</u>, and increases the reader's <u>sympathy</u> for the monster.

3) The monster takes <u>refuge</u> from "the barbarity of man" in a "<u>hovel</u>" attached to a <u>cottage</u>. He calls it "a <u>paradise</u> compared to the <u>bleak</u> forest".

> **Theme — Prejudice**
>
> The <u>monster</u> experiences prejudice because he's judged by his <u>appearance</u>, rather than on his <u>inner worth</u> — see p.41 for more.

The monster watches the De Lacey family

1) The <u>family</u> who live in the cottage, the De Laceys, behave with "love and respect", in <u>contrast</u> to everybody the monster has seen so far.

2) By <u>paying</u> "perpetual attention" to the De Laceys, the monster begins to <u>understand</u> some of their speech. He also secretly gathers <u>wood</u> to help them — showing that he can be <u>empathetic</u> and <u>kind</u>.

3) The monster <u>realises</u> that he's <u>ugly</u>, and his "miserable <u>deformity</u>" makes him feel "<u>despondence</u>". He seems to share humanity's <u>prejudice</u> against himself — when he sees his reflection he's <u>convinced</u> he's a "<u>monster</u>".

4) He plans to learn to <u>talk</u> so that the family will <u>overlook</u> his <u>appearance</u>. His "hope and anticipations of joy" create <u>uneasiness</u>, since the reader has already seen the <u>prejudiced</u> nature of humans in the novel.

© ITV/REX

Talk about how the monster's story creates sympathy...

Shelley has already hinted that Frankenstein isn't blameless in the deaths so far. The monster's perspective helps to shift some more blame in that direction, as his wretched loneliness causes us to pity him.

Analysis of Chapters 13 and 14

The De Lacey family have a complicated history, which conveniently includes a non-French-speaking love interest called Safie. They teach Safie their language, and inadvertently teach the monster to speak too.

The monster begins to learn about how society works

1) Safie arrives at the De Laceys' home, and the monster learns to speak French by secretly listening to the lessons the De Laceys give her. He learns more quickly than Safie, and is eager to be taught.

2) Felix reads a history book to Safie, and from it the monster learns about human history. He's appalled at the evil that "noble and godlike" humans can do, which shows his innocent and idealistic nature.

3) By learning about human history, the monster realises that he has nothing that would make society value and accept him. He has "no money, no friends, no kind of property", and he thinks that he'll be seen as "a blot upon the earth".

4) The monster wishes he'd never found out what an outcast he is. He was happier before he gained this knowledge, but it "clings to the mind" — he can't regain his lost innocence.

Theme — Prejudice

Safie is different and an outsider, but the De Laceys accept her into their family. This gives the monster hope that they won't be prejudiced against him, but he's still rejected.

Theme — Knowledge

Like Frankenstein, the monster has a hunger for knowledge. However, the more he learns, the more disillusioned he becomes with humanity. It also makes him aware of his lonely existence.

The monster becomes aware of his loneliness

1) The monster realises he's never experienced family bonds or love, which emphasises his loneliness. It also reminds the reader that Frankenstein has failed to act as a parent to the monster.

2) The monster calls the people in the cottage his "friends" and "protectors", which shows how alone he is — the De Laceys are his only friends in the world, and they don't even know he exists.

3) The monster says bitterly that he saw them as friends in an "innocent, half-painful self-deceit", which shows the monster's naivety, and hints at his later rejection.

© Moviestore Collection/REX

The De Lacey story highlights problems in society

In Chapter 14 the monster learns about the history of the De Lacey family and Safie. Shelley uses the De Laceys' past to present some messages about society:

- Safie's father experienced prejudice — he was an outsider, who was persecuted for being wealthy and a Muslim. His unjust arrest is an example of corruption in society.

- Safie's mother taught her "independence of spirit", which causes her to reject her father's authority. She's the only female character in the novel who's able to fully take control of her own life, and Shelley portrays her rebelliousness in a positive way.

KEY QUOTE *"sorrow only increased with knowledge"*

The more the monster learns, the more he starts to realise that humans aren't necessarily the nicest of creatures. He doesn't heed these warnings though — he still thinks he'll be able to befriend the De Laceys.

Section Two — Discussion of Chapters

Analysis of Chapters 15 and 16

The monster finally decides to introduce himself to his new 'friends'... let's just say it doesn't go well.

Reading makes the monster even more miserable

1) The monster finds three <u>books</u> in a nearby <u>wood</u>. The *Sorrows of Werter* makes the monster <u>question</u> his own <u>existence</u> — "Who was I? What was I?" — as well as making him see the differences between himself and other people. *Plutarch's Lives* makes the monster admire "<u>virtue</u>" and hate "<u>vice</u>".

2) *Paradise Lost* has the <u>biggest</u> effect on the monster. He identifies himself with <u>Adam</u>, because he's the <u>first</u> of a new <u>species</u>, but he realises that, unlike himself, Adam is happy and protected by his creator. The monster also identifies with Satan because he feels "<u>envy</u>" over the perfect lives of other humans.

3) The monster also <u>reads</u> Frankenstein's <u>journal</u>, which teaches him about the "<u>disgusting</u> circumstances" of his <u>origin</u>. He calls Frankenstein his "<u>Accursed</u> creator!" and <u>questions</u> why Frankenstein made him — echoing the words of Adam in *Paradise Lost*, which are quoted on *Frankenstein's* <u>title page</u> (see p.8).

The monster reveals himself

KEY EVENT

1) The monster decides to <u>reveal</u> himself to De Lacey when he's alone. The monster hopes that his <u>blindness</u> will mean that he won't be <u>prejudiced</u> against him.

2) De Lacey is <u>sympathetic</u> to the monster and offers him help. However, when the <u>rest of the family</u> arrive home they react with <u>horror</u> at the sight of the monster, and Felix viciously <u>attacks</u> him.

3) The monster won't <u>fight</u> Felix, but he rampages through the forest "like a <u>wild</u> beast". When he returns to the cottage and finds it empty he burns it down, symbolising the <u>destruction</u> of his only link with <u>society</u>.

> <u>Rejection</u> makes the monster act like the terrifying <u>beast</u> that everyone expects him to be.

The monster murders William

1) The monster <u>travels</u> to Geneva to <u>find</u> his <u>creator</u>. On the way there he's <u>shot</u> after <u>saving</u> a child from <u>drowning</u>. After this, the monster vows "eternal <u>hatred</u> and <u>vengeance</u> to all <u>mankind</u>".

2) Despite this, the monster approaches William in the hope that someone so <u>young</u> will be "<u>unprejudiced</u>", and might still want to be his <u>friend</u>. However, William reacts with <u>terror</u>.

3) The monster <u>kills</u> William when he finds out that he's <u>related</u> to <u>Frankenstein</u>, and feels "exultation and hellish triumph" at his act. Shelley shows that repeated <u>rejection</u> by society has meant that <u>hatred</u> has replaced the monster's natural <u>goodness</u>. The monster then <u>frames</u> Justine for the <u>murder</u>.

4) The monster ends his story by <u>demanding</u> that Frankenstein make him a <u>companion</u>. He tells Frankenstein that he "must" create a companion for him to end his <u>loneliness</u>.

> **Theme — Prejudice**
>
> The monster is <u>prejudiced</u> against Justine — he automatically <u>assumes</u> that she would "denounce" him if she woke up.

EXAM TIP

Look for similarities between the different narratives...

The monster and Frankenstein are both on downward spirals — they begin life with curiosity, hope and the ability to love, but by the end of each narrative, they're both consumed by hatred and revenge.

Analysis of Chapters 17 to 20

Frankenstein reluctantly agrees to make a girlfriend for the monster, but he then has a change of heart and destroys her. The monster is not exactly thrilled by this turn of events...

The monster is eloquent but threatening

© Alastair Muir/REX

1) The monster argues <u>persuasively</u> that he's only "<u>malicious</u>" because human <u>prejudice</u> has made him so "<u>miserable</u>".

2) However, in-between being "<u>reasonable</u> and <u>moderate</u>", the monster makes <u>threats</u>. He <u>warns</u> Frankenstein that if he can't "inspire <u>love</u>" then he'll "cause <u>fear</u>".

3) Frankenstein feels some <u>compassion</u> for the monster, but <u>hatred</u> quickly overcomes him. In the end, however, he sees the "<u>justice</u>" in the monster's argument, and <u>agrees</u> to make him a companion if he promises to <u>disappear</u> afterwards.

Frankenstein's decision makes him more isolated

1) Frankenstein returns <u>home</u>, and promises to <u>marry</u> Elizabeth. Inwardly, however, he reacts with "<u>horror</u> and <u>dismay</u>", and decides that he <u>can't</u> marry her until his business with the monster is <u>finished</u>.

2) Frankenstein travels with Clerval through Europe to Britain, with the <u>secret</u> intention of talking to some <u>scientists</u> to gain the <u>knowledge</u> he needs to make a female monster.

3) Unlike Clerval, Frankenstein doesn't <u>enjoy</u> the trip — for example, he sees Edinburgh with "languid eyes and mind", and is in "no mood" to <u>socialise</u> with the people they meet in Scotland.

4) The <u>beauty</u> of the <u>nature</u> around them makes Clerval "<u>joyful</u>", but Frankenstein can't <u>appreciate</u> it — he's "<u>haunted</u> by a curse that shut up every avenue to <u>enjoyment</u>". Unlike before, nature can't <u>improve</u> how Frankenstein feels.

Theme — Isolation

Frankenstein's decision to create another monster makes him want to <u>isolate</u> himself. The monster's demands make him <u>lonely</u>.

Writer's Techniques — Setting

In Chapter 5, Frankenstein's return to health is helped by a "<u>divine spring</u>" which "<u>contributed greatly</u>" to his <u>recovery</u>, but now nature has <u>less power</u> to restore him.

Frankenstein changes his mind about the new monster

1) After <u>delaying</u> it for as long as he can, Frankenstein eventually starts to build the <u>new monster</u> in a hut in the Orkneys. However, one night he decides that his <u>decision</u> to create a female monster is <u>selfish</u> — he thinks he might be putting the <u>safety</u> of "the whole human race" at <u>risk</u> by creating her.

2) The monster <u>appears</u> at the window, and Frankenstein <u>destroys</u> the female monster as he <u>watches</u>. The monster reacts with "<u>devilish</u> despair", and <u>threatens</u> "I shall be with you on your <u>wedding-night</u>".

3) Frankenstein goes out in a <u>boat</u> and gets rid of the female monster's <u>remains</u>, but then a <u>storm</u> blows him off course. He reaches a "<u>small neat town</u>" but his <u>relief</u> is short-lived, as he's <u>arrested</u> for murder.

"You are my creator, but I am your master; — obey!"

Frankenstein and the monster constantly wrestle for power. One minute the monster's winning, the next he's powerless to stop the destruction of his girlfriend. But the monster's about to take charge in a big way...

Analysis of Chapters 21 and 22

An eye for an eye, a tooth for a tooth, a best friend for a freaky zombie monster. It's the way of the world...

Frankenstein is wrongly accused of Clerval's murder

1) Frankenstein eventually finds out that the <u>murder</u> that he was <u>arrested</u> for was that of his <u>best friend</u>, Henry Clerval, and he falls <u>ill</u>. It's clear to Frankenstein that Clerval was murdered by the monster.

2) Although Frankenstein is innocent, he still feels guilty because he was indirectly <u>responsible</u> for Clerval's death. When he's <u>ill</u>, he calls himself "the <u>murderer</u> of William, of Justine, and of Clerval".

3) Frankenstein's <u>language</u> becomes very similar to the monster's — for example, he says he's "the most miserable of mortals". Shelley does this to show how the monster's actions are making Frankenstein more <u>lonely</u> and <u>miserable</u> — mirroring what Frankenstein's actions have done to the monster.

4) However, Frankenstein still <u>benefits</u> from <u>human support</u>. Frankenstein's father arrives to help him and he sees him as a "<u>good angel</u>". The magistrate, Kirwin, is "<u>benevolent</u>" and shows Frankenstein "extreme <u>kindness</u>".

> **Theme — Prejudice**
>
> Despite believing he's <u>guilty</u> of <u>murder</u>, the townspeople give Frankenstein <u>shelter</u> and <u>food</u> while he's <u>ill</u>. This contrasts with the monster's <u>treatment</u> in the novel — even when he hasn't done anything <u>wrong</u>, his <u>appearance</u> means that he gets no <u>help</u> from anybody.

5) Frankenstein is acquitted, but it doesn't make him feel better — he says that "the <u>cup of life</u>" is "<u>poisoned</u> forever", and it's only his desire to <u>protect</u> his remaining loved ones that stops him from committing <u>suicide</u>.

The wedding creates a sense of tension

1) After reading a letter from Elizabeth, Frankenstein remembers the monster's <u>threat</u> — "I will be with you on your wedding-night!" It's repeated twice more in Chapter 22, creating an <u>ominous atmosphere</u>.

2) Frankenstein compares himself and Elizabeth to <u>Adam and Eve</u>, about to be forced out of <u>Eden</u> — "the <u>apple</u> was already <u>eaten</u>, and the <u>angel's</u> arm bared to drive me from all <u>hope</u>". He also says that the monster is "<u>invincible</u>" and "<u>omnipotent</u>", which implies he's as powerful as a god. This <u>reverses</u> the monster's words in Chapter 10, when he said that he should've been Frankenstein's "Adam".

> **Writer's Techniques**
>
> Frankenstein and the monster have <u>switched</u> roles — Frankenstein has gone from being '<u>God</u>' (in Chapter 10) to being '<u>Adam</u>', and the monster is now <u>god-like</u>. This implies that the monster has the <u>power</u> in their relationship.

3) Shelley <u>skims over</u> the description of Elizabeth and Frankenstein's <u>wedding</u> — this keeps the <u>mood</u> of the novel as <u>tragic</u> and <u>dark</u> as possible.

4) Elizabeth has a "<u>presentiment</u> of evil" — she seems to <u>know</u> that something <u>bad</u> is about to happen. Frankenstein is also <u>anxious</u> and <u>on edge</u>. He has a "prophetic feeling", and arms himself with "pistols and a dagger".

5) Frankenstein describes the boat trip to Evian after their wedding as his "<u>last</u> moments" of <u>happiness</u>. The sun sets, creating an <u>ominous</u> sense of <u>finality</u> and <u>darkness</u>.

Look out for hints in the text before bad events occur...

Don't forget — Frankenstein is narrating this story with hindsight, knowing exactly what's going to happen and when. He drops lots of hints before anything bad happens in order to increase the tension in the novel.

Analysis of Chapters 23 and 24

These are the last few chapters of Frankenstein's narrative — and they're not cheerful ones.

The monster kills Elizabeth in revenge

Frankenstein assumes the monster's threat (see p.18) means that he'll try to kill him on his wedding night, not Elizabeth.

1) Frankenstein paces around <u>anxiously</u> as he waits for the monster. This creates <u>tension</u>, which is <u>echoed</u> by the "<u>restless</u> waves" on the lake, and the clouds, which move "<u>swifter</u> than the flight of the vulture".

2) Frankenstein hears a <u>scream</u>. His <u>body</u> feels "<u>suspended</u>" — this <u>contrasts</u> with the <u>motion-filled</u> build-up of the scene, and <u>prepares</u> the reader for something <u>shocking</u>.

3) The monster's <u>grinning face</u> at the <u>window</u> is a <u>reminder</u> of his appearance in <u>Scotland</u>, when Frankenstein <u>destroyed</u> the female monster. By killing Elizabeth, the monster takes <u>revenge</u> on Frankenstein for that act, and condemns him to the same <u>loneliness</u> that he suffers.

© Alastair Muir/REX

Frankenstein and the monster are bound to each other by hatred

1) Frankenstein's father, who has provided <u>support</u> for him throughout his life, dies of grief.

2) Frankenstein then tries to get help from a <u>magistrate</u> to catch the monster, but he fails and is forced to seek <u>revenge</u> on his own.

3) Throughout the novel, Shelley reduces the <u>differences</u> between Frankenstein and the monster. Like the monster, Frankenstein has become <u>friendless</u>, and he can't get help from <u>society</u> (i.e. the magistrate). Frankenstein's language is also full of intense <u>loathing</u> — he says revenge is the "devouring and only passion of my soul".

4) As Frankenstein pursues the monster, they're <u>linked</u> together by hate — the monster <u>gloats</u> that Frankenstein's <u>suffering</u> can "<u>satisfy</u>" his "everlasting hatred". In a way, he has got the <u>companion</u> he wanted, but it's a relationship built on <u>hate</u>, not <u>love</u>.

> **Writer's Techniques — Imagery**
>
> Frankenstein carries "<u>eternal hell</u>" with him, <u>echoing</u> the monster's words in Chapter 16 ("I... bore a hell within me"). This <u>biblical imagery</u> links them to <u>Satan</u>, and it shows the misery and hatred they feel.

Frankenstein is driven by powerful forces

1) Frankenstein's <u>desire</u> for <u>revenge</u> is "like a mighty tide" and he's "possessed" by <u>rage</u>. He's able to endure great hardships — his <u>determination</u> to <u>catch</u> the monster <u>matches</u> his earlier determination to <u>create</u> him.

2) Shelley casts <u>doubt</u> over Frankenstein's <u>sanity</u>. Frankenstein begins to lose touch with reality, and he sees <u>ghosts</u> — "the spirits of the dead hovered round and instigated me to toil and revenge".

3) When Frankenstein reaches the <u>end</u> of his story, he <u>begs</u> Walton to <u>kill</u> the monster if Frankenstein <u>dies</u> before he gets the chance. He's still <u>convinced</u> of the <u>evil</u> nature of the <u>monster</u> — he says that his "soul is as hellish as his form, full of treachery and fiendlike malice".

KEY QUOTE

"it is the devouring and only passion of my soul"

Remember when science was Frankenstein's one true love? Seems like he's changed his mind now — this quote's about revenge, not science. After losing everyone he loves, all he has left to motivate him is hate.

Analysis of 'Walton, in continuation'

The narrative returns to Walton as the novel comes to an end.

Walton still sees Frankenstein as a noble, tragic figure

1) Walton's opinion of Frankenstein as an "admirable being" reminds the reader of what potential Frankenstein had at the beginning of his narrative. It makes the waste of his life seem more tragic.

2) Frankenstein seems to be doomed to die — Walton says that he's found the friend he wanted, only to "know his value and lose him". His descriptions show the broken state Frankenstein is in — exhausted, weak and feverish, and talking to his dead family as if they were alive.

3) Despite Frankenstein's story, Walton remains passionate about his voyage — "I had rather die than return shamefully — my purpose unfulfilled". His recklessness shows that he hasn't recognised the warning in Frankenstein's story.

Frankenstein hasn't changed his mind

1) Frankenstein examines his "past conduct", and decides that he's not "blamable" for what has occurred.

2) Frankenstein believes that his "duties" towards mankind were more important than his duty to the monster — but he ignores the fact that once he'd created the monster, it was his duty to help and protect him.

3) Even as Frankenstein dies, he's still undecided about the dangers of ambition and the knowledge he sought. He tells Walton to "avoid ambition", but then questions himself — "Yet why do I say this?... another may succeed". Despite the tragedy he's suffered, he can't let go of his ambition and obsession with knowledge.

> **Theme — Ambition**
>
> Shelley presents Frankenstein as unable to learn from his mistakes, and Walton is reluctant to turn back. This suggests that mankind will never learn from the dangers of over-ambition.

The monster shows remorse

> **Writer's Techniques**
>
> Walton describes the monster's ugliness as "unearthly", and it causes him to shut his eyes "involuntarily". Shelley implies that people have an instinctive fear and loathing of the unnatural monster.

1) After Frankenstein dies, Walton sees the monster mourning over his corpse. He's shocked by his "loathsome yet appalling hideousness".

2) The monster hates himself and acknowledges his guilt. He reminds Walton that he was capable of "love and sympathy" but was "wrenched by misery to vice and hatred" — leaving the reader feeling more sympathetic towards him.

3) The monster also calls himself an "abortion", reminding us that he's unwanted, as well as implying that he wasn't really meant to be alive in the first place.

4) The monster tells Walton that, now that Frankenstein is dead, he will commit suicide. Shelley implies that the monster has nothing left to live for — his hatred for Frankenstein was the only thing driving him.

© JONES Pete/ArenaPAL

"Seek happiness in tranquillity and avoid ambition"

Especially if your ambition gets you a walking, talking, murdering monster. Frankenstein seems to have learnt his lesson at the end, but then he goes and contradicts himself. This shows he's not really changed.

Practice Questions

You knew it was coming — it's time for some more questions, this time on the ins-and-outs of the novel's plot. Again, for the quick questions on this page, just jot down a few words or a sentence — you can save those juicy longer answers for the next page.

Quick Questions

1) Where is Walton trying to travel to at the beginning of the novel?

2) Find a quote that explains why Walton wants to have a friend.

3) What was Frankenstein's childhood like?

4) Who arrives in Ingolstadt immediately after Frankenstein creates the monster?

5) Why doesn't Frankenstein tell the truth about the monster after Justine's arrest?

6) How does Frankenstein react when he meets the monster for the first time?

7) How does the monster learn to speak French?

8) Why does the monster think that De Lacey will listen to him?

9) Why does Frankenstein travel to Britain?

10) What happens to Frankenstein after he disposes of the female monster's remains?

11) What happens to Alphonse Frankenstein?

12) What does the monster decide to do after Frankenstein's death?

Practice Questions

Good news — there's only one more page of questions to go before you've checked off another section of the book, which means you're one step closer to being an all-round 'Frankenstein' mastermind. First, though, have a stab at these longer questions — a paragraph will do nicely for the in-depth questions, and then tackle the exam-style questions as if you were actually in an exam.

In-depth Questions

1) Explain why Professor Waldman is important in the novel.

2) What does Justine's death suggest about the law and justice in *Frankenstein*? Find some quotes to support your answer.

3) How does Shelley make the monster appear vulnerable in Chapter 11?

4) To what extent does the monster's eloquence help him in the novel?

5) How is Safie's arrival at the De Laceys' cottage important in the monster's life?

Exam-style Questions

1) Read the passage in Chapter 10 that begins "'I expected this reception,'..." and ends "'Make me happy, and I shall again be virtuous.'"

   Using this extract, discuss how Shelley presents the relationship between Frankenstein and the monster in *Frankenstein*.
   Write about:
   a) the way it's presented in this extract, and
   b) the way it's presented in the novel as a whole.

2) "Frankenstein is wholly responsible for the deaths of William and Justine." To what extent do you agree with the above statement?

3) Read the passage in Letter 2 that starts "But I have one want..." and ends with "...endeavour to regulate my mind."

   Discuss the way that Shelley presents friendship in the novel. You should talk about the above extract in your answer, as well as the rest of the book.

Character Profile — Victor Frankenstein

Frankenstein is kind of a big deal — he's the one with his name on the front cover of the book. Talking about him in the exam is pretty much a given, so make sure you spend some time getting to grips with his character.

Frankenstein has an obsessive desire for knowledge

1) Frankenstein is a young man with a <u>passionate interest</u> in studying <u>science</u> — he has "ardently desired the acquisition of <u>knowledge</u>" since childhood.

2) He's capable of "intense application", which earns him "great esteem" as a student. His <u>enthusiasm</u> for "discovery and wonder" presents his scientific interest in a <u>positive</u> light.

3) However, Frankenstein's <u>love of science</u> becomes an <u>obsessive ambition</u> to bring inanimate matter to life. This leads him to do a lot of very <u>disturbing</u> things (see p.37), and when he succeeds in creating the monster, he causes a lot of <u>damage</u>:

- In the <u>short term</u>, he becomes <u>unwell</u> for several months after the monster's creation.
- In the <u>long term</u>, he causes the <u>suffering</u> and <u>deaths</u> of himself and others.

He can be self-absorbed

1) Frankenstein's obsession makes him <u>neglectful</u> of his family — he rarely writes and doesn't visit them for several years when at university.

2) He's so <u>obsessed</u> with his moment of <u>scientific glory</u> that he doesn't consider what he'll do with his creation afterwards. He's <u>relieved</u> when the monster vanishes — it doesn't occur to him that it might be his <u>responsibility</u> to look after the monster.

> **Frankenstein is...**
>
> **Passionate**: "engaged, heart and soul, in the pursuit of some discoveries".
>
> **Ambitious**: "I will pioneer a new way, explore unknown powers".
>
> **Self-centred**: "no creature had ever been so miserable as I was".

3) Frankenstein often presents himself as a <u>victim</u>:

- Frankenstein describes his "<u>unparalleled</u> misfortunes" — he thinks <u>nobody</u> has suffered as much as him, despite the misery and death that his <u>family</u> have endured. This makes him seem <u>self-centred</u>.

- He often blames <u>fate</u> for his situation, saying that <u>destiny</u> has decided his "utter and terrible destruction". He feels that his misery was <u>unavoidable</u>.

- Frankenstein's focus on the role of <u>destiny</u> in his life suggests that he's unable to take responsibility for his actions. He could also be trying to make his story seem more <u>favourable</u> to Walton.

4) Frankenstein presents himself as a <u>tragic hero</u> — a character with a <u>fatal flaw</u> that causes their <u>downfall</u>. He describes his ambition as a "fatal impulse" that led to his "ruin".

5) Shelley leaves it up to the <u>reader</u> to <u>decide</u> whether he's a self-absorbed man who can't take responsibility for his actions, or if he's a tragic hero and a victim of fate.

> **Background and Context**
>
> Frankenstein presents himself as someone who suffers the consequences of trying to <u>benefit humanity</u>, like <u>Prometheus</u> (see p.8).

Character Profile — Victor Frankenstein

Frankenstein is surrounded by people who love him

1) Frankenstein is <u>supported</u> and <u>loved</u> by the people around him:

© ITV/REX

- His <u>parents</u> adore him with "inexhaustible stores of <u>affection</u>", and Alphonse comes to <u>rescue</u> him from Ireland.

- Clerval nurses him through <u>illness</u>, suggesting that he's <u>dedicated</u> to Frankenstein.

- Elizabeth feels a "<u>sincere</u>" love for Frankenstein, despite his physical and emotional <u>distance</u>.

- Even Walton, who meets Frankenstein when he's at his <u>weakest</u>, loves him "as a brother", and <u>cares</u> for him when he's dying.

2) In return, Frankenstein <u>loves</u> his friends and family <u>deeply</u>. The monster understands this, so he deliberately kills those <u>closest</u> to Frankenstein to inflict the <u>most pain</u> on him.

3) However, Frankenstein's love for those closest to him <u>can't match</u> his <u>passion</u> for science or for revenge. The <u>help</u> and <u>love</u> that his friends and family give him <u>strongly contrasts</u> with his <u>neglect</u> of them.

He becomes physically and mentally weaker

1) Even <u>before</u> he creates the monster, Frankenstein is very <u>emotional</u>. As a child, for example, his "temper was sometimes violent" and his "passions vehement" (intense).

2) As his narrative progresses, he <u>changes</u> from being happy and loved to being isolated and unbalanced.

- As a child, he has "bonds of the closest <u>friendship</u>" with Clerval, and is in "harmony" with Elizabeth. Later, his obsession and his guilt make him <u>withdrawn</u>. He says he "<u>shunned</u>" society and found company "irksome".

- <u>Physically</u>, he gets increasingly <u>unwell</u>, becoming "a shattered <u>wreck</u>" and a "shadow of a human being".

- By the time he meets Walton he's <u>unbalanced</u> — he talks to the "spirits of the dead" as if they're <u>real</u>, and Walton sees a "wildness" in his eyes.

At the end of his life he's deeply troubled

Writer's Techniques — Language

<u>Revenge</u> becomes the focus of Frankenstein's language as well. Early in the novel, <u>science</u> was his "sole occupation", but now revenge is his "<u>only</u> passion".

1) Frankenstein's single-minded <u>ambition</u> eventually leads to a single-minded quest for <u>revenge</u>, his "devouring and only <u>passion</u>".

2) Meanwhile, he can no longer decide whether or not it's right to <u>pursue</u> <u>ambition</u> — he tells Walton to "avoid ambition", but makes a <u>passionate</u> <u>speech</u> to persuade Walton's crew to continue on their voyage north.

3) On his deathbed, Frankenstein is aware that he may be "<u>misled</u> by passion". However, he then thinks that the pursuit of knowledge can be a <u>good thing</u> — saying that another "may <u>succeed</u>" where he has failed.

EXAM TIP

Think about Frankenstein's morality...

Readers are divided over Frankenstein — some people think he's a horrible guy for abandoning the monster, but others are more sympathetic. Make sure you can back up <u>your</u> opinion with evidence from the text.

Character Profile — The Monster

The monster is definitely a two-sided character — he has some sympathetic aspects to his personality, and he's treated badly by society, but that teeny tiny 'brutal murderer' issue just keeps getting in the way...

The monster is naturally inclined to be good

1) The monster's first appearance in the novel is written from Frankenstein's perspective. Frankenstein's "breathless <u>horror</u> and <u>disgust</u>" makes the monster seem <u>repulsive</u>. He's also described as a "<u>fiend</u>", which makes him seem <u>threatening</u>.

2) Later, Shelley uses the monster's own narrative to force the reader to <u>rethink</u> this initial impression. The monster is clearly <u>vulnerable</u> because he <u>knows so little</u> — he describes himself as "a poor, helpless, miserable wretch". He's also <u>treated brutally</u> by the <u>first</u> people he meets, which presents him as pitiful, and suggests that he's a <u>victim</u>.

3) Shelley also presents the monster as <u>naturally good</u>, which evokes the reader's sympathy:

> - His <u>childlike innocence</u> at the sight of the "miraculous" village is <u>endearing</u>, and suggests that he's inclined to see things in a <u>positive</u> light.
>
> - He shows he's <u>considerate</u> by secretly collecting <u>wood</u> for the De Laceys and clearing <u>snow</u> from their path.
>
> - He <u>empathises</u> with the <u>emotions</u> of the De Lacey family — "when they rejoiced, I <u>sympathised</u> in their joys".
>
> - He's <u>hopeful</u> — despite his <u>bad treatment</u> by others, he continues to try to <u>engage</u> with people. Even after the De Laceys' rejection, he tries to save a girl from drowning.

4) Shelley uses the monster's narrative to show that he was <u>not born evil</u>. He's presented in a <u>sympathetic</u> way that makes him seem more <u>endearing</u> to the reader.

The monster is...

Lonely: "I alone am irrevocably excluded".

Bitter: "All men hate the wretched".

Vengeful: "I will work at your destruction".

Theme — Isolation

The monster is referred to in many different ways throughout the novel, but he <u>never</u> gets a <u>real name</u>, emphasising how much of an <u>outsider</u> he is.

Background and Context

This reflects the ideas of Jean-Jacques <u>Rousseau</u>, who believed that all people are born <u>naturally</u> innocent, then <u>corrupted</u> by society (see p.7).

The monster's treatment changes him

1) The monster's <u>rejection</u> by society makes him <u>angry</u> and <u>bitter</u>. Frankenstein's neglect "<u>sickened</u>" him and made him feel "<u>hatred</u>", whilst the rejection of the <u>De Laceys</u>, who were his "only link" to the world, causes him to feel "a rage of <u>anger</u>".

2) The monster says he was "wrenched by <u>misery</u> to vice and hatred", drawing the reader's attention to other characters' <u>responsibility</u> for his change.

3) <u>Rejection</u> eventually leads the monster to seek <u>revenge</u> on Frankenstein.

© KINGWILL Marilyn/ArenaPAL

The monster is angry at Frankenstein's failure to take <u>responsibility</u> for him. However, the monster doesn't take any <u>moral responsibility</u> for the murders he commits, which is <u>hypocritical</u>. He even asks Frankenstein how he can dare to "sport... with life", when he himself has killed William.

Character Profile — The Monster

The monster's revenge is ruthless

1) The monster's <u>aggression</u> is <u>terrifying</u> — he threatens <u>evil</u> that will swallow up "thousands" in the "whirlwinds of its rage".

2) He <u>revels</u> in the <u>pain</u> he inflicts on Frankenstein, and he murders William "with <u>exultation</u> and hellish <u>triumph</u>" — although he later feels "<u>despair</u>" at the act he's committed.

3) The monster's revenge is <u>brutal</u>. He makes Frankenstein suffer a <u>worse punishment</u> than <u>death</u>, by killing his loved ones and then making him "drag out" his "weary existence" alone. He wants to cause Frankenstein <u>as much pain as possible</u>.

Background and Context

The monster decides that since he can't be <u>happy</u>, he will <u>cause suffering</u> instead — "Evil thenceforth became my good". In *Paradise Lost*, Satan says "Evil be thou my good" — Shelley uses language to draw <u>parallels</u> between the two characters.

© ITV/REX

Theme — Revenge

The monster learns about <u>revenge</u> from other people. Shelley could be suggesting that revenge is part of <u>human nature</u>, and that by seeking revenge the monster is actually becoming more <u>human</u>.

The monster is linked with Frankenstein

1) The monster and Frankenstein have <u>similarities</u> in their <u>personalities</u>:

Intelligent	⇒	They both seek <u>knowledge</u> — the monster feels "wonder and <u>delight</u>" when he learns to read.
Obsessive	⇒	Their determination for <u>revenge</u> spurs them on, and drives them to their <u>deaths</u>.
Isolated	⇒	Isolation is <u>forced</u> upon the monster, whilst Frankenstein's <u>loneliness</u> is initially his <u>choice</u>.

2) As the story <u>continues</u>, the monster seems to have more in <u>common</u> with his <u>creator</u>. Like Frankenstein, he becomes obsessed with his own "superior" <u>suffering</u>, and at the end of the novel he says he's "torn by the bitterest remorse". Despite the fact that they're <u>enemies</u>, Shelley suggests that the monster and Frankenstein are ultimately <u>not that different</u>.

3) In some ways, the <u>relationship</u> between Frankenstein and the monster <u>reverses</u>. Towards the end of the novel, the monster says he's Frankenstein's "<u>master</u>". This shows that the monster has gained <u>power</u> over Frankenstein, which is also demonstrated by the way he <u>leads</u> Frankenstein north — <u>guiding</u> him with taunting messages.

Writer's Techniques — The Gothic Novel

The monster acts as Frankenstein's <u>double</u> (or <u>doppelgänger</u>), which a key element of the <u>Gothic genre</u>. See p.51 for more.

KEY QUOTE

"I was benevolent and good; misery made me a fiend."

The monster's actions lead to quite a few deaths in the novel, and we probably can't forgive him for that. But Shelley does want us to see that other people are at least partly responsible for the person he becomes.

Character Profile — Robert Walton

Ambitious, swashbuckling sea captain seeks intelligent male with GSOH for bromance on long sea voyage. Must have cultivated and ambitious mind. Interest in conferring an inestimable benefit on mankind preferred.

Walton is adventurous but also lonely

1) Walton is the first character to be introduced in the novel. He's an ambitious polar explorer, who's trying to fulfil his dream of travelling to the North Pole.

2) Walton is idealistic — he imagines the North Pole as "a land surpassing in wonders", even though he knows it's dangerous.

3) He's compassionate — he feels "sympathy and compassion" for Frankenstein, and tells his sister that he's safe so she won't worry.

4) Walton is also lonely. He feels "bitterly" affected by his lack of friends — his voyage has made him isolated (see p.40).

© Moviestore Collection/REX

Walton is a lot like Frankenstein...

1) Frankenstein and Walton have lots of similarities in their personalities and pasts:

- Walton's ambition mirrors Frankenstein's — he's driven to explore by "ardent curiosity" and, like Frankenstein, he believes that he'll "benefit" mankind.

- He can sound reckless — he says that he would sacrifice "fortune" and "existence" for success. Similarly, Frankenstein insists Walton's crew should continue north despite the dangers they face.

- Walton prepared for his expedition with sea voyages and extensive studying. He's as obsessive and hardworking as Frankenstein is.

- Walton was inspired by the books he "read with ardour" (love) when he was younger. Frankenstein's love of science was also inspired by books he read with "delight" as a child .

2) Because of their similarities, Walton acts as a warning to the reader that Frankenstein's problems are not unique — there are other men like Frankenstein in the world.

... but unlike Frankenstein, Walton's fate isn't sealed

Walton is one of the novel's narrators — see p.46 for more on this.

1) Despite Frankenstein's warning, Walton doesn't want to give up on his ambition — he thinks it shows "cowardice and indecision", and that returning home is an "injustice".

2) However, he does abandon his voyage, and he heads back to England at the end of the novel. Ultimately, he doesn't descend into ruin like Frankenstein does because he recognises the dangers of continuing his quest.

Robert Walton is...

Confident: "success *shall* crown my endeavours".

Ambitious: "I shall satiate my ardent curiosity".

Sensitive: "his... deep grief fills me with sympathy and compassion".

KEY QUOTE

"What can stop the determined heart... of man?"

Walton is a bit like an early Frankenstein, before things went wrong. Despite Frankenstein's cautionary tale, though, Walton doesn't change his views on ambition — he's unhappy about abandoning his mission.

Character Profile — Henry Clerval

Frankenstein's best pal, Henry Clerval, is attractive, selfless and terrifyingly enthusiastic. The sort of person you'd like to have around in times of crisis, but wouldn't be able to stand at half six on a Monday morning.

Clerval is a foil to Frankenstein

1) Henry Clerval is Frankenstein's <u>school friend</u>. They grow up together, but their lives eventually follow very <u>different paths</u>.

2) Clerval is <u>intelligent</u> and <u>ambitious</u>, like Frankenstein. He eventually persuades his father to let him go to Ingolstadt to <u>study</u>, and as a child he loves "enterprise, hardship, and even danger".

3) However, his <u>ambitions differ</u> from Frankenstein's — Elizabeth teaches him to aim for "doing good".

4) Shelley presents Clerval as the person Frankenstein <u>could</u> have become if he hadn't been so <u>obsessive</u> and <u>isolated</u> — Frankenstein says that in Clerval he saw the "image" of his "former self". He acts as Frankenstein's <u>foil</u>.

> **Henry Clerval is...**
> **Cheerful:** "I enjoy existence!"
> **Generous:** "so thoughtful in his generosity".
> **Romantic:** "The scenery of external nature... he loved with ardour".

A foil is a character who shares similarities, but also some important differences, with another character. This emphasises each character's key characteristics.

Clerval is uplifted by the world around him

1) The stories that Clerval <u>loves</u> as a child are tales of <u>chivalry</u> and <u>selflessness</u>. As an adult, his friendships make him "glad", and he puts Frankenstein's needs <u>before</u> his own, which demonstrates his selfless nature.

2) He learns <u>languages</u>, and plans to travel the world and meet people, suggesting that he's <u>sociable</u>. This <u>contrasts</u> with Frankenstein, who only travels so that he can learn more about <u>science</u>.

3) Clerval greatly appreciates the <u>natural world</u> — when he's in Europe, he sees the nature around him with an "eye of feeling and <u>delight</u>".

Chivalry is the code of conduct by which medieval knights lived.

> **Background and Context**
> Shelley refers to the <u>stories</u> of "the Round Table of King Arthur" and "the heroes at Roncesvalles". These legends <u>focus</u> on the importance of <u>heroic</u> behaviour.

> **Background and Context**
> Clerval's appreciation of <u>nature</u> links him with 'Romantic' ideas about nature's power to inspire intense <u>emotions</u>. See p.7.

His company is good for Frankenstein

1) Clerval's cheerful presence in Ingolstadt makes Frankenstein feel "<u>calm</u> and <u>serene</u> joy", and his "<u>affection</u> warmed and opened" Frankenstein's senses. He also <u>reconnects</u> Frankenstein with <u>society</u>, persuading him to write to his <u>family</u>.

2) Alphonse and Elizabeth recognise the <u>positive effect</u> Clerval has on Frankenstein and arrange for him to accompany Frankenstein to Britain.

3) Clerval's <u>importance</u> in Frankenstein's life is <u>emphasised</u> by Frankenstein's reaction to his death. He's <u>physically sickened</u> by it — he suffers "strong convulsions". He tells Walton that he still feels "parched with horror" when he thinks of Clerval's death — making it seem more <u>tragic</u>.

© ITV/REX

You can compare Clerval with Frankenstein...

Clerval and Frankenstein have grown up together, but they've become very different people over time. Clerval shows the reader what Frankenstein could've been like, if he hadn't been so obsessed with science.

Character Profile — Elizabeth Lavenza

Another scarily perfect (but doomed) companion for Frankenstein — and he marries this one.

Elizabeth is family-orientated

1) Elizabeth was <u>adopted</u> at a young age by the Frankensteins, and raised as part of their <u>family</u>.

2) She has a strong sense of <u>maternal responsibility</u>. When Frankenstein's mother, Caroline, <u>dies</u>, Elizabeth carries out her <u>dying request</u> to look after the "younger children". She <u>hides</u> her grief and tries to <u>comfort</u> her family.

3) After Justine dies, Elizabeth believes that family <u>love</u> will help them through the <u>tragedy</u> — as long as they stay <u>true</u> to one another, she questions "what can disturb our <u>peace</u>?"

© SNAP/REX

She's presented as an idealised woman

1) Frankenstein <u>idealises</u> Elizabeth, emphasising what he sees as her best qualities. She's <u>contented</u>, <u>home-loving</u> and <u>loved</u> by others with a "passionate and almost reverential attachment".

2) She has a <u>positive influence</u> on everyone around her. She made Frankenstein less "sullen" and more <u>gentle</u>, and inspired Clerval to be "perfectly <u>humane</u>".

3) However, Shelley presents Elizabeth as being <u>too perfect</u> for the corrupt world she lives in, making her death seem <u>inevitable</u>. Shelley <u>foreshadows</u> Elizabeth's death after Justine's conviction, when Elizabeth says that she "<u>cannot live</u> in this world of misery".

Elizabeth Lavenza is...

Loving: "She was the living spirit of love".
Beautiful: "fairer than pictured cherub".
Selfless: "She forgot even her own regret".

Writer's Techniques — Language

Shelley uses <u>religious language</u> to emphasise Elizabeth's <u>purity</u> and <u>virtue</u>. Elizabeth is "<u>heaven-sent</u>", and she has a "<u>saintly</u>" soul.

She is a victim of Frankenstein's actions

1) Elizabeth's happiness is <u>dependent</u> on Frankenstein's. Even though she loves him, she says that their marriage would make her miserable if he was <u>unhappy</u>. This <u>dependence</u> on a man who can be reckless and self-centred makes her <u>vulnerable</u>.

2) She's presented as <u>belonging</u> to Frankenstein — Caroline describes her as "a pretty <u>present</u>" for him, and he refers to her as "<u>mine</u>". This emphasises the <u>control</u> Frankenstein has over her.

3) Frankenstein's <u>actions</u> eventually result in Elizabeth's <u>death</u>.

Background and Context

Elizabeth and Frankenstein's <u>relationship</u> highlights the <u>patriarchal</u> (male-dominated) attitudes of the time. Most women were <u>completely dependent</u> on their families or husbands.

- When Elizabeth is murdered she's presented as an <u>innocent</u> victim. She's "<u>worthy</u>" even in death.

- Elizabeth's <u>physical appearance</u> is drastically changed in death — she has "<u>distorted</u> features", and has "ceased to be... Elizabeth". This makes her death seem more <u>shocking</u> and <u>unpleasant</u>.

KEY QUOTE

"fairer than a garden rose amongst dark-leaved brambles"

Elizabeth is more than just pretty — she's loving, caring, virtuous and so sweet it makes your teeth ache. However, the world is full of "brambles" — not the ideal place for a "garden rose". Bye bye, Lizzie.

Character Profile — Frankenstein's Parents

Loving parents — but predictably, they're doomed too. Is it just me, or is there a pattern emerging here?

Alphonse values family and society...

1) Frankenstein's father is a "Syndic" (a magistrate) in Geneva. He has a strong sense of social duty and puts his faith in society and its institutions. He believes he can "rely on the justice" of the law to find William's murderer — although he's proven wrong by the outcome of Justine's trial.

2) He cares about his family. After William's murder, he shows more concern for Frankenstein's feelings than his own grief. The gradual destruction of his family breaks his heart, eventually causing his death.

3) Alphonse also values friendship — for example, he seeks out Caroline's father in order to help him, and cares for Caroline after her father dies.

© ITV/REX

...as does his wife, Caroline

1) Caroline was loyal and supportive to her sick father. She attended him "with the greatest tenderness" and worked hard to bring in money.

2) She's caring and affectionate towards her children, and feels "beloved" by her family. Some of Frankenstein's earliest memories are of his "mother's tender caresses".

3) Caroline also contributes to society. It's her "passion" to help the poor, remembering how she was once "an orphan and a beggar". She adopts Elizabeth from a poor family, and treats her with love and generosity.

4) She dies of scarlet fever after selflessly nursing Elizabeth through sickness. She's brave when she's dying, trying to "resign" herself "cheerfully" for the sake of her family.

Caroline's selflessness and maternal nature provide a parallel with Elizabeth's.

Theme — Creation

Caroline is Frankenstein's birth mother, so she represents natural motherhood and creation.

Frankenstein doesn't always appreciate his father

1) Frankenstein implies that Alphonse is partly responsible for his interest in unusual science. Alphonse dismissed Frankenstein's books on natural philosophers as "sad trash", but didn't explain why — so Frankenstein studied them with more enthusiasm.

2) Frankenstein ignores Alphonse's advice not to seek revenge for William's death, which might have saved him from destruction. He also doesn't visit his father whilst he's at university, or turn to him for help.

Character — The Monster

Shelley highlights the absence of a parental figure in the monster's life by using Alphonse and Caroline as a contrast. Frankenstein fondly remembers Caroline's "tender caresses", but the monster becomes aware that "no mother" had "blessed" him with "smiles and caresses".

For more on families in the novel, see p.39.

EXAM TIP

Think about parent figures in the story...

Alphonse and Caroline are important — they're Frankenstein's parents, and Frankenstein himself is a kind of parent to the monster. His neglect of the monster contrasts with the good example his parents set him.

Character Profile — William and Justine

Justine... that sounds a lot like justice... and Justine/justice is killed due to prejudice. Nice symbolism, Mary.

Justine behaves admirably but suffers injustice

1) Justine is the Frankenstein family's servant. She's <u>rejected</u> by her mother, but is <u>welcomed</u> into the Frankenstein family, and treated with <u>respect</u>.

2) Justine is framed for William's <u>murder</u> as she sleeps. After her trial she falsely <u>confesses</u> for fear of going to <u>hell</u> — the priest "threatened" and "menaced" her until she almost believed she was a "<u>monster</u>".

3) Justine is described as being like an "<u>affectionate mother</u>" to William and, when he goes missing, she <u>searches</u> for him all night. This shows her <u>loyalty</u> and <u>kindness</u> to the Frankenstein family and makes her conviction for William's murder seem more <u>unjust</u>.

4) Despite this <u>injustice</u>, she's <u>brave</u> and dignified. She "<u>repressed</u> her bitter <u>tears</u>" and "assumed an air of <u>cheerfulness</u>" to try to make Frankenstein and Elizabeth feel better.

5) Shelley presents Justine as a <u>vulnerable</u> character, who doesn't <u>deserve</u> the injustice that she suffers.

> **Theme — Prejudice**
>
> Like the monster, Justine suffers prejudice — she's executed for William's murder on <u>circumstantial evidence</u>. The priest calling her a "<u>monster</u>" emphasises this <u>parallel</u>.

> **Theme — Family**
>
> Like Caroline and Elizabeth, Justine is another <u>selfless</u>, <u>maternal</u> figure in the novel.

William is the monster's first victim

1) Frankenstein's youngest brother, "darling William", is <u>loved</u> by his whole family, and even the monster says William never injured "any other living thing". This makes his murder seem more <u>shocking</u>.

2) The monster <u>hopes</u> William is <u>too young</u> to have "a <u>horror</u> of deformity", but William judges him like everyone else. Shelley suggests that even the <u>youngest</u> people in society can still be <u>prejudiced</u>.

> **Background and Context**
>
> William is initially presented as the '<u>Romantic</u>' ideal of an <u>innocent</u>, uncorrupted child. However, it turns out that he's <u>prejudiced</u> too. Shelley could be <u>questioning</u> this idealised presentation of childhood.

William and Justine are significant to the plot

1) William's death is the monster's first act of revenge, and he realises that hurting Frankenstein's <u>family</u> will "torment and destroy" him.

2) Frankenstein calls Justine's death the "<u>miserable epoch</u> from which I dated all my woe". Frankenstein can <u>never forgive</u> the monster for William and Justine's deaths, which:

An 'epoch' is a distinctive point in time.

- leads to the monster and Frankenstein becoming "<u>enemies</u>".
- triggers Frankenstein's <u>refusal</u> to make another monster.
- creates a cycle of <u>revenge</u> that leads to more <u>deaths</u>.

© ITV/REX

Comment on the impact of William and Justine's deaths...

William's and Justine's are the first of a string of monster-related deaths in the novel. Their deaths set off the cycle of revenge between Frankenstein and the monster, which causes even more death and destruction.

Character Profile — The De Laceys and Safie

The De Laceys are the monster's one shot at a proper family, and at one point it even seems like they might be kind enough to understand him and welcome him in. No such luck...

The De Laceys seem perfect but are prejudiced

1) The De Laceys are an exiled French family, who the monster observes whilst he's in hiding.

2) They're presented as the model of a loving, selfless family. The children, Felix and Agatha, secretly give up their food for their father, and perform "every little office of affection and duty with gentleness".

3) De Lacey, the father of the family, is a virtuous man, who's "respected by his superiors and beloved by his equals". He supported Felix's plan to put right an injustice, despite the potential danger and personal cost.

4) Felix has a strong sense of justice. He feels uncontrollable "horror and indignation" when Safie's father is persecuted, and he gives himself up in the hope of saving his father and sister from prison.

5) However, despite his good qualities, Felix judges the monster instantly, and beats him "violently". This vicious reaction to the monster shocks the reader, and evokes sympathy for the monster.

> Because he's blind, De Lacey judges the monster on his sincere speech rather than his appearance — he's the only character who doesn't reject the monster immediately. De Lacey believes people are "full of brotherly love and charity", but his confidence seems idealistic after Felix attacks the monster.

Character — Alphonse

De Lacey is very similar to Alphonse — they both have integrity and are supportive of their children. They're both dedicated fathers, emphasising what the monster is missing out on.

Theme — Prejudice

The De Lacey family are presented as "superior beings", but even they react with horror to the monster. This emphasises how deeply-rooted prejudice is in human society.

© ITV/REX

Safie is an accepted outsider

1) Safie is a beautiful Turkish woman, who comes to live with the De Lacey family after her father escapes from the law. She's Felix's lover, but they have been separated for a period of time.

2) She's been raised to value "independence" by her mother, so she rebels against her father before he can take her to Turkey to live in a harem. Safie is the only female character in the novel who takes control over her own life.

3) Safie's relationship with Felix is romantic — he's "ravished with delight" by her and she's "always gay and happy" with him. Shelley uses their interaction to highlight another type of love that the monster is denied.

Theme — Society and Isolation

Shelley marks Safie as different to the De Laceys in culture and language, but they still accept her. This contrasts with their attitude to the monster, emphasising his isolation.

KEY QUOTE

"They did not appear rich, but they were contented and happy"

The De Laceys are an idealised loving family — it isn't poverty that makes them sad, it's losing Safie. Their story shows the importance of both family and romantic love, both of which the monster is denied.

Practice Questions

Ease yourself in gently with a nice box of quick questions — just scribble down about a sentence for each one. After that, there are some in-depth questions to really get your cogs turning. Remember to have a flick back through the section if you get stuck.

Quick Questions

1) Name two damaging effects, one short term and one long term, of the creation of the monster.

2) Give one example from the text that suggests the monster is:
   a) good
   b) evil

3) Find a quote which suggests that Walton is reckless.

4) Give one way in which Clerval's company is good for Frankenstein.

5) Find two quotes where Shelley describes Elizabeth using religious language.

6) Give one example of a time when Caroline cares for others.

7) Find a quote that suggests William is innocent.

8) Find a quote from the text that suggests the De Laceys are:
   a) prejudiced
   b) loving

In-depth Questions

1) Briefly explain the similarities between Walton and Frankenstein.

2) Do you think Alphonse is a good father? Explain your answer.

3) Explain some of the ways in which Shelley presents Justine as a sympathetic character.

4) How does Shelley use Safie to emphasise the monster's isolation?

Practice Questions

Here's a page full of fiendish-looking exam-style questions. Don't tackle all of these in one go so that you can spend a decent chunk of time and effort on each one, and try to treat them like the real thing — so turn off the telly, set yourself a time limit, pick up your favourite pen and get stuck in.

Exam-style Questions

1) Explore the importance of the character of Robert Walton in *Frankenstein*.

2) Using the extract below as a starting point, explain how Shelley presents the character of the monster in *Frankenstein*.

Taken from Chapter 10

As I said this, I suddenly beheld the figure of a man, at some distance, advancing towards me with superhuman speed. He bounded over the crevices in the ice, among which I had walked with caution; his stature, also, as he approached, seemed to exceed that of man. I was troubled; a mist came over my eyes, and I felt a faintness seize me; but I was quickly restored by the cold gale of the mountains. I perceived, as the shape came nearer (sight tremendous and abhorred!) that it was the wretch whom I had created. I trembled with rage and horror, resolving to wait his approach, and then close with him in mortal combat. He approached; his countenance bespoke bitter anguish, combined with disdain and malignity, while its unearthly ugliness rendered it almost too horrible for human eyes. But I scarcely observed this; rage and hatred had at first deprived me of utterance, and I recovered only to overwhelm him with words expressive of furious detestation and contempt.

"Devil," I exclaimed, "do you dare approach me? And do not you fear the fierce vengeance of my arm wreaked on your miserable head? Begone, vile insect! Or rather, stay, that I may trample you to dust! And, oh! That I could, with the extinction of your miserable existence, restore those victims whom you have so diabolically murdered!"

"I expected this reception," said the dæmon. "All men hate the wretched: how, then, must I be hated, who am miserable beyond all living things! Yet you, my creator, detest and spurn me, thy creature, to whom thou art bound by ties only dissoluble by the annihilation of one of us. You purpose to kill me. How dare you sport thus with life? Do your duty towards me, and I will do mine towards you and the rest of mankind. If you will comply with my conditions, I will leave them and you at peace; but if you refuse, I will glut the maw of death, until it be satiated with the blood of your remaining friends."

---

3) *"I, with childish seriousness, interpreted her words literally, and looked upon Elizabeth as mine — mine to protect, love, and cherish."* (Victor Frankenstein)

Using this quote as a starting point, explore the significance of the relationship between Elizabeth and Frankenstein in the novel.

4) Have a look at the passage in Chapter 11 that begins "On examining my dwelling..." and ends "... they entered the cottage together."

Discuss how Shelley presents Safie and the De Laceys in the novel.
Write about:
a) The way the De Lacey family are presented in this passage, and
b) The way that Safie and the De Laceys are presented in the novel as a whole.

Knowledge and Ambition

Knowledge and ambition are huge themes in *Frankenstein* — it's Frankenstein's scientific ambition that gets the plot moving. Might've been a whole different book if he'd had an all-consuming passion for cross-stitch.

Walton and Frankenstein both ambitiously seek knowledge

1) Frankenstein and Walton both have a <u>passion</u> for <u>learning</u> and making new <u>discoveries</u>.

2) They're motivated by lifelong <u>ambitions</u> — Frankenstein has had "a lofty <u>ambition</u>" since he was a boy, and Walton's voyage was the "favourite <u>dream</u>" of his childhood.

3) To an extent, their ambitions are <u>noble</u>, because they both want to benefit mankind. Frankenstein intends to use <u>knowledge</u> about the human body to "banish <u>disease</u>", and Walton thinks that his voyage will be of "inestimable <u>benefit</u>" to mankind.

> **Writer's Techniques — Symbolism**
>
> Shelley uses images of <u>light</u> to represent <u>new knowledge</u> (see p.48). Walton calls the North Pole a "country of eternal light" and Frankenstein wants to "pour a torrent of light" into the world. This positive imagery emphasises the <u>potential benefits</u> of their discoveries.

4) However, Shelley also hints at a <u>selfish</u> side to their ambitions — Walton says he "preferred <u>glory</u>" to all else, and Frankenstein is excited by the idea that a new species would "<u>owe</u> their being" to him.

5) Shelley doesn't present <u>new discoveries</u> in a completely <u>negative</u> way, but the novel does suggest that when the pursuit of certain types of knowledge is <u>combined</u> with selfish <u>ambition</u>, it can be dangerous.

> **Character — Henry Clerval**
>
> Shelley presents another side to <u>ambition</u> through Henry Clerval. His ambition isn't presented as <u>dangerous</u> because it's <u>controlled</u> and <u>unselfish</u> — with Elizabeth's influence, "doing good" is the "end and aim of his soaring ambition".

Ambition causes destruction in the novel

Shelley presents ambition as a <u>destructive</u> force:

> **It causes harm to the people who pursue it...**
>
> • Frankenstein becomes <u>ill</u> when he makes the monster. He grows "pale", loses <u>weight</u> and suffers from a "<u>nervous fever</u>" after he first sees his creation.
>
> • Frankenstein and Walton are both <u>isolated</u> by ambition — Walton needs a friend "<u>bitterly</u>" and Frankenstein becomes gradually more <u>withdrawn</u> (see p.40).

© Moviestore Collection/REX

> **... and it causes harm to the people around them**
>
> • Walton's ambitions make him <u>reckless</u>. Several of his sailors die from the "excessive" cold, yet he's still willing to risk the <u>lives</u> of everyone on his ship by wanting to continue travelling north.
>
> • Frankenstein's ambition ends up being very <u>destructive</u> to other people — he <u>releases</u> a monster into the world, which brings about the deaths of his <u>friends</u> and <u>family</u>.

Knowledge and Ambition

Shelley warns that some knowledge is forbidden

Charnel houses are buildings where bones are kept.

1) The <u>knowledge</u> that Frankenstein pursues is presented as <u>disturbing</u> — he "<u>tortured</u>" animals, he spends "<u>days and nights</u>" in charnel houses and he describes the "<u>horrors</u>" of his "filthy creation".

2) It's also presented as <u>violent</u>. Shelley uses <u>battle imagery</u> when Frankenstein describes his scientific work:

- Frankenstein says that he wanted to destroy the "<u>fortifications</u>" that the "citadel of nature" had put up — as if nature is the <u>enemy</u> in a <u>battle</u>.

- He says he wants to "break through" the bounds of "Life and death", and pursue "nature to her hiding-places" — it's as if he's marching into new <u>territory</u> and <u>plundering</u> it. This emphasises the <u>relentless</u> nature of his ambition.

Writer's Techniques — Imagery

Shelley also uses <u>biblical imagery</u> to suggest that pursuing some types of knowledge is <u>sinful</u>. Frankenstein compares his search for knowledge to a "serpent", referring to the story of <u>Adam and Eve</u>, in which Satan appears as a snake and <u>persuades</u> Eve to disobey God by eating the <u>forbidden</u> fruit from the tree of <u>knowledge</u>.

3) Shelley's language suggests that the type of <u>knowledge</u> Frankenstein pursues is <u>forbidden</u> and <u>dangerous</u> because his work causes him to clash with <u>nature</u>.

Gaining knowledge damages the monster

1) The monster is <u>disillusioned</u> by knowledge, and sometimes wishes that he'd never acquired it. The more he learns about <u>human society</u>, the more he realises that people will never <u>accept</u> him.

2) The De Lacey family's history teaches the monster about human <u>virtues</u>, but also about the "<u>vices</u> of mankind" — this makes him more <u>cynical</u>.

3) He learns language and <u>reads</u> Frankenstein's <u>journals</u>, where he discovers the <u>disgust</u> his creator feels for him. He's "sickened" and calls Frankenstein his "<u>Accursed creator!</u>" — this anger eventually leads him to <u>murder</u> and <u>destruction</u>.

Background and Context

Shelley may be suggesting that it's <u>better</u> for mankind to live in a natural state, where organised <u>society</u> doesn't exist. This links to the ideas of the philosopher <u>Jean-Jacques Rousseau</u> (see p.7).

Shelley makes suggestions about human nature

1) Using Walton and Frankenstein's stories, Shelley presents mankind's tendency to <u>ambitiously overreach</u> as both <u>self-destructive</u> and <u>repetitive</u>.

2) Frankenstein shows that some people <u>don't learn</u> from their own mistakes. Even as he's <u>dying</u> from the results of his discoveries, Frankenstein still believes in the <u>possibilities</u> of science. He thinks that someone else "may <u>succeed</u>" where he has <u>failed</u>.

3) Through Walton, Shelley suggests that humans may be <u>doomed</u> to <u>repeat</u> the mistakes of others — despite Frankenstein's story, Walton is <u>reluctant</u> to give up on his expedition.

© JONES Pete/ArenaPAL

KEY QUOTE *"sorrow only increased with knowledge"*

The monster's experiences seem to suggest that the more we learn, the more difficult things get.
(CGP Disclaimer: "I didn't want to increase my sorrow" is not an acceptable excuse to avoid revising.)

Creation

It's pretty clear from the way Shelley writes that she was a <u>big</u> fan of all things natural and lovely. In contrast, the monster is presented as something *un*natural, which emphasises his disturbing, inhuman existence.

Natural creation is a positive influence in the novel...

1) The natural world is presented as <u>beautiful</u> — Shelley describes "the beauties of nature" throughout the novel (see p.50).

2) Shelley also links the natural world with <u>God</u>. Frankenstein is reminded of "a power mighty as <u>Omnipotence</u>" (God) when he visits the Alps, and Clerval describes the river Rhine as "divine".

3) Shelley suggests that the natural world can <u>restore</u> people. When Frankenstein sees how <u>small</u> he is in comparison to the "eternity" of the Alps, it makes his problems feel <u>less significant</u>, and he feels that the "<u>weight</u>" of his sorrows is "<u>lightened</u>".

> **Background and Context**
>
> '<u>Romantic</u>' writers believed that the <u>natural</u> world was a <u>reflection</u> of God's <u>perfection</u>, which offered human beings a chance to <u>appreciate</u> God's power. They also believed that nature had <u>restorative effects</u>.

... but the monster is an unnatural creation

1) Frankenstein's <u>ambition</u> is to create life using science, <u>without</u> involving a woman. This is an <u>unnatural</u> form of <u>creation</u>.

2) When Frankenstein is creating the <u>monster</u>, he shuts himself <u>away</u> from "a most beautiful season" in his "workshop of filthy creation". His <u>withdrawal</u> from the <u>natural world</u> suggests that his task is <u>unwholesome</u>.

> When Frankenstein meddles with <u>unnatural creation</u>, he becomes <u>less affected</u> by nature's restorative powers. By the time he's about to create the <u>second monster</u>, his enjoyment of nature is "<u>embittered</u>".

3) Frankenstein describes the monster as "hideous". He's failed to <u>imitate</u> God, who made Adam "a <u>perfect</u> creature".

4) The monster is created with parts from "the unhallowed damps of the <u>grave</u>" — raiding <u>graves</u> was considered particularly <u>blasphemous</u> at the time (see p.6). The monster is created out of <u>death</u>, and that's exactly what he causes.

5) Shelley suggests that meddling in <u>unnatural creation</u> and upsetting the <u>laws of nature</u> is dangerous, ungodly and should be avoided.

Blasphemous means disrespectful to God.

© Everett Collection/REX

Character — The Monster

> Despite being an unnatural creation, the monster is very <u>human</u> in many ways. His desire to give and receive <u>love</u> is a <u>natural human instinct</u>. However, he's <u>denied</u> love, and the opportunity to give love, and this makes him inhumane and monstrous. He says "If I have no ties and no affections, hatred and vice must be my portion".

KEY QUOTE

"I kept my workshop of filthy creation"

Frankenstein is meddling with things he shouldn't be. Shelley presents creation as the domain of God — you could look at the events of the novel as a kind of consequence for messing around with life and death.

Family

There are lots of family relationships in the novel — some of them are more dysfunctional than others...

Family bonds can be healthy and supportive

1) Families are presented as an important source of <u>happiness</u> and <u>support</u>. Frankenstein's <u>parents</u> recognise their <u>duties</u> towards their children:

- **Love** — they give Frankenstein "inexhaustible stores of <u>affection</u>".

- **Support** — Alphonse ensures that Frankenstein doesn't go on his travels <u>alone</u> by making Clerval join him, and he <u>travels</u> to Ireland to <u>support</u> Frankenstein when he's in jail.

- **Education** — Frankenstein is taught "patience" and "self-control" by his parents, but he <u>doesn't</u> live by these qualities once he <u>leaves</u> his family. This suggests that a parent's example can be <u>important</u>, and needs reinforcing.

2) The De Lacey family provide another <u>model</u> of family <u>love</u>. The monster thinks they're "<u>superior</u> beings" because of the way they behave with <u>consideration</u> and <u>loyalty</u> to each other.

Women often have motherly values

1) Caroline Frankenstein <u>prioritises</u> family — she makes <u>sacrifices</u> in order to take care of her dying father, and she thinks about her children even when she's <u>dying</u> herself.

2) Caroline also <u>expands</u> her family — she <u>adopts</u> Elizabeth and <u>takes in</u> Justine.

3) Elizabeth treats her younger "cousins" like her <u>children</u>. She talks about William as if he's her <u>son</u>, calling him "my little William", and takes Caroline's place in the family after she dies.

Women in the Frankenstein family follow the same pattern. They suffer <u>hardships</u>, then are <u>taken in</u> by the family and become motherly <u>role models</u> — Elizabeth assumes the role of a mother to William and Ernest, and Justine is an "affectionate <u>mother</u>" to William. Women are crucial to <u>holding a family together</u>.

There are also examples of bad families in the novel

1) Some of the family relationships in *Frankenstein* are <u>less healthy</u>, e.g. Justine's mother <u>doesn't love her</u>. Elizabeth describes this as a "strange perversity", suggesting she considers it <u>unnatural</u> not to love a child.

2) Despite their presentation as an ideal family, the De Laceys <u>reject</u> the monster from their family unit. <u>Supportive</u> family love is presented as <u>important</u>, which makes the monster's lack of family seem more <u>tragic</u>.

3) Frankenstein <u>created</u> the monster, so he's effectively his <u>father</u> and only <u>parent</u>, but he refuses to raise him. Without family love, the monster becomes <u>bitter</u> and <u>angry</u> — which leads to <u>tragedy</u>.

Frankenstein says that his life was his parents' <u>responsibility</u>, "to direct to happiness or misery". The fact that his life ends in <u>tragedy</u> could suggest that even Alphonse and Caroline have made <u>mistakes</u> raising their children.

Write about the role of families in the novel...

OK, so Frankenstein won't be winning Parent of the Year any time soon, but there would be a few other nominees. Mention how the loving family relationships in the novel make Frankenstein's neglect stand out.

Society and Isolation

Society in Frankenstein certainly has some benefits, but it's also got more flaws than a multi-storey car park...

Society benefits most of the characters

1) In the novel, society is shown to have <u>two main functions</u> (although there's some <u>overlap</u> between them):

   - To provide <u>company</u> and <u>friendship</u>, such as Frankenstein's friendship with Clerval.
   - To provide wider <u>support</u>, both through social <u>institutions</u> like the Church and the law, and through members of a town or village <u>community</u> supporting one another.

   Rousseau wrote about the effects of society on an individual. See p.7.

2) Frankenstein's <u>friendship</u> with Clerval gives him <u>joy</u> and <u>strength</u>, and he believes that a good friend can "perfectionate our weak and faulty natures".

3) Caroline feels it's a "necessity" to <u>help</u> the poor in society, and Felix made a "solemn vow" to help Safie's father, despite not <u>knowing</u> him. Shelley shows how members of a society can <u>support</u> one another.

But Shelley highlights society's problems as well

1) Society is presented as <u>imperfect</u> in *Frankenstein*. The <u>violent</u> reactions to the monster show that <u>human groups</u> can be aggressive and <u>prejudiced</u> (see p.41).

2) <u>Poverty</u> is also a <u>problem</u> — Caroline's father dies in <u>shame</u> after he loses his wealth, and Elizabeth's <u>poor</u> foster family are "bent down by care and labour". Society seems to create this <u>inequality</u>.

3) Shelley also suggests that society's <u>institutions</u> can <u>fail</u> people. Justine is bullied by a member of the <u>Church</u> and executed by a court of <u>law</u> even though she's <u>innocent</u>, which Frankenstein calls a "wretched mockery of justice".

Writer's Techniques

The monster learns about the <u>failings</u> of society during his narrative. Shelley forces the reader to see society from an <u>outsider's perspective</u> in order to highlight its problems.

The novel explores the impact of isolation

Isolation has a big <u>impact</u> on some characters in the novel:

Walton — Walton is <u>physically</u> isolated by his ambitions, and he <u>longs</u> for a <u>friend</u>. He calls it a "severe evil" that he has nobody to "sympathise" with him — his isolation makes his voyage <u>less satisfying</u>.

Frankenstein — Frankenstein <u>chooses</u> to isolate himself, but when he's alone with his work he's often <u>miserable</u> and <u>unhealthy</u>. By the time he makes the female monster, even Clerval's friendship <u>can't relieve</u> his "miserable fears". This shows how <u>damaging</u> extreme isolation can be.

Monster — The monster's isolation is <u>involuntary</u>. Society offers him <u>no support</u>, either through friendship or through social institutions and community. This makes him <u>malicious</u>, and he begins to use his loneliness as a <u>weapon</u>, punishing Frankenstein by inflicting the <u>same loneliness</u> on him.

© ITV/REX

EXAM TIP — ***Talk about different causes of loneliness...***

Frankenstein's isolation is often his choice — he doesn't like being around people when he's absorbed in his work, or feeling guilty. But the monster doesn't get to choose — he's alone whether he likes it or not.

Prejudice

I'm not sure if you noticed, but people in the novel tend to be a *teensy* bit uncomfortable around the monster. I can sympathise with them — and you would too if you'd met my great-auntie Edna...

Society is prejudiced against the monster

© Everett Collection/REX

1) Frankenstein describes the moment the monster awakes as a "catastrophe". He immediately judges the monster on his ugly appearance.

2) Other people also react negatively towards the monster's appearance, even when he's performing a heroic deed like saving a girl from drowning. He's never allowed the chance to prove his inner worth.

> Prejudice affects the monster more than it affects any other character in the novel. It shapes his personality and the course of his life.

3) De Lacey is blind, so he's the only person who doesn't judge the monster. Instead, he highlights the monster's other qualities, such as eloquence — the way he speaks persuades De Lacey that he's sincere.

4) The prejudice the monster suffers teaches him how to be prejudiced himself:

- The monster is prejudiced against humanity as a whole — he vows "vengeance to all mankind" and claims that "All men hate the wretched". He believes that all people are the same.

- This prejudice leads him to frame Justine, because he assumes that she shares the prejudices of everyone else he's met.

- The monster also starts to believe in society's prejudiced opinion of him, and begins to loathe himself. He's "terrified" by his reflection in a pool, and becomes "convinced" that he's a "monster".

Other characters also experience prejudice

1) Aside from prejudice against the monster, there are other examples of prejudice in the novel:

- Walton shows class prejudice — he desperately wants a friend, but he assumes that he won't find one among "merchants and seamen".

- Justine is condemned to death unfairly. Frankenstein criticizes the prejudice of the court system, claiming that "public indignation" was turned against her.

- Safie's father also suffers discrimination at the hands of the law. He's sentenced to death by a court because of his religion.

- Frankenstein is a victim of prejudice in Ireland, when he's arrested for Clerval's murder without evidence.

> Shelley suggests that prejudice can turn people into monsters — it leads people to treat Justine cruelly, and it drives the monster to murder.

2) Justine confesses because she's almost persuaded that she really is a "monster". This links the prejudice against Justine to the prejudice that the monster suffers.

 KEY QUOTE

"Shall I not then hate them who abhor me?"

Prejudice doesn't just make the monster evil — it also makes him a) hate himself, and b) prejudiced against innocent people like Justine. Remember that there are other prejudices in the novel as well.

Revenge

Frankenstein pursues the monster all the way to the icy Arctic in an attempt to avenge the deaths of his family and friends. Well, they do say revenge is a dish best served cold...

Revenge drives Frankenstein and the monster

1) The monster <u>begins</u> the <u>cycle</u> of revenge in the novel. He <u>kills</u> William to <u>punish</u> Frankenstein — he realises it'll "create desolation" for him.

2) Revenge <u>sustains</u> both Frankenstein and the monster. The monster's desire for revenge becomes "dearer than light or food" to him. Vengeance also becomes Frankenstein's only <u>reason</u> to live.

3) Frankenstein and the monster's obsession for revenge binds them <u>together</u>, which is represented physically by their "<u>pilgrimage</u>" to the Arctic.

Character — The Monster

The monster's revenge is calculated, demonstrating his <u>intelligence</u>. For example, instead of killing Frankenstein on his wedding night, he kills Elizabeth, knowing this will <u>hurt</u> Frankenstein <u>deeply</u>.

© Moviestore Collection/REX

Writer's Techniques

A "pilgrimage" is usually a <u>religious</u> journey. Shelley suggests that Frankenstein has become as devoted to <u>revenge</u> as someone might be to <u>religion</u>.

Shelley shows that revenge is not healthy or satisfying

1) Revenge is presented as an <u>unhealthy</u> obsession. Alphonse <u>begs</u> Frankenstein to <u>avoid</u> "brooding thoughts of <u>vengeance</u>" after William's death, as they end up "festering the wounds of our minds". This suggests that revenge is like a <u>disease</u>.

2) Frankenstein admits that revenge is a "<u>vice</u>", but it becomes the "devouring and only <u>passion</u>" of his soul. It <u>isolates</u> him permanently from society and drives him to the Arctic, eventually leading to his <u>death</u>.

3) Revenge doesn't <u>satisfy</u> the characters. For example, the monster says that revenge has been "deadly <u>torture</u>" to him and has made him <u>miserable</u>.

4) It takes Frankenstein's death to <u>break</u> the cycle of revenge, which prompts the monster to ask for <u>forgiveness</u> for everything he's done. But it's too late, and whilst the monster achieves the <u>destruction</u> he wanted, he's still left <u>unsatisfied</u> and he feels that he now has nothing left to live for.

Character — Frankenstein

Frankenstein comes to see his <u>revenge</u> as a "task enjoined by <u>heaven</u>". This shows how <u>obsession</u> has <u>distorted</u> his values — he's stopped seeing his search for the monster as simply a quest for <u>revenge</u>, and has started to believe that he's carrying out a <u>divine duty</u>.

Writer's Techniques

Shelley links the themes of <u>ambition</u> and <u>revenge</u> together. She presents revenge as selfish and all-consuming, and it leads to <u>isolation</u> and <u>misery</u> in the same way ambition does.

KEY QUOTE *"my hatred and revenge burst all bounds of moderation"*
Revenge is dangerous and powerful — both the monster's and Frankenstein's lives go significantly downhill as they get wrapped up in a big, messy spiral of revenge and anger. It's all rather dramatic, isn't it?

Practice Questions

More practice questions! Get cracking with these lovely theme-based questions, which should help you remember everything you've learnt in this chapter. Speed through these and you'll find... yes, more questions.

Quick Questions

1) Find a quote which suggests that Frankenstein's ambition is:
   a) selfish
   b) unselfish

2) Give two examples from the novel that show that ambition is destructive.

3) Name a type of imagery that Shelley uses to present Frankenstein's pursuit of knowledge as either forbidden or dangerous.

4) Give two ways in which knowledge damages the monster.

5) Why is the monster an unnatural creation?

6) Write down two things that Alphonse and Caroline provide for their family.

7) Give an example of a bad family relationship in the novel.

8) Suggest a character who helps others in their society, and write down how they achieve this.

9) Name two characters who are upset by their lack of a friend.

10) Why isn't De Lacey immediately prejudiced against the monster?

11) Aside from the monster, name two characters who suffer prejudice in the novel.

12) Who is the first character to attempt revenge?

Practice Questions

Now that you're nicely warmed up, how about a few in-depth questions? Remember, your answers to these need to be a bit longer, and back up what you say with some quotes and examples.

In-depth Questions

1) Do you think ambition is presented in a positive or negative way in the novel? Use examples from the text to explain your answer.

2) What does Shelley's presentation of ambition suggest about human nature?

3) Explain how Shelley presents natural creation in a positive way.

4) How does Frankenstein's relationship with nature change as he meddles with unnatural creation?

5) Do you think the De Lacey family are an admirable family? Support your answer with examples from the text.

6) Briefly explain how Shelley presents society as flawed in the novel.

7) How does isolation affect the monster? Find evidence from the text to support your answer.

8) In what ways could the monster be considered a prejudiced character?

9) Briefly explain how revenge is a driving force in the novel.

10) "Shelley presents revenge as pointless." Do you agree with this statement? Support your answer with examples from the text.

Practice Questions

Sharpen your pencils and stock up on biscuits — it's time for the big ones. I know it sounds obvious, but you don't want the first exam answer you write to be the one in the exam itself. If you familiarise yourself with the kinds of questions you'll face in the exam now, then you'll be much more relaxed on the day.

Exam-style Questions

1) Read the extract in Chapter 13 that begins "Every conversation of the cottagers..." and ends "...a state which I feared yet did not understand."

   Write about Shelley's presentation of knowledge as harmful in *Frankenstein*.
   In your answer you should refer to both the extract and the novel as a whole.

2) "*I have no friend, Margaret: when I am glowing with the enthusiasm of success, there will be none to participate my joy; if I am assailed by disappointment, no one will endeavour to sustain me in dejection.*" (Robert Walton)

   Using this quote as a starting point, explore the importance of friendship in the novel.

3) To what extent is prejudice the reason that the monster is evil?

4) Discuss how Shelley presents the theme of revenge in *Frankenstein*.

   Write about:
   a) How revenge is presented in the extract below, and
   b) How revenge is presented in the novel as a whole.

   Taken from Chapter 24

   The deep grief which this scene had at first excited quickly gave way to rage and despair. They were dead, and I lived; their murderer also lived, and to destroy him I must drag out my weary existence. I knelt on the grass and kissed the earth, and with quivering lips exclaimed, "By the sacred earth on which I kneel, by the shades that wander near me, by the deep and eternal grief that I feel, I swear; and by thee, O Night, and the spirits that preside over thee, to pursue the dæmon who caused this misery, until he or I shall perish in mortal conflict. For this purpose I will preserve my life; to execute this dear revenge will I again behold the sun and tread the green herbage of earth, which otherwise should vanish from my eyes for ever. And I call on you, spirits of the dead; and on you, wandering ministers of vengeance, to aid and conduct me in my work. Let the cursed and hellish monster drink deep of agony; let him feel the despair that now torments me."

   I had begun my abjuration with solemnity and an awe which almost assured me that the shades of my murdered friends heard and approved my devotion, but the furies possessed me as I concluded, and rage choked my utterance.

   I was answered through the stillness of night by a loud and fiendish laugh. It rung on my ears long and heavily; the mountains re-echoed it, and I felt as if all hell surrounded me with mockery and laughter. Surely in that moment I should have been possessed by frenzy, and have destroyed my miserable existence, but that my vow was heard and that I was reserved for vengeance.

Structure, Narrative and Form

Frankenstein is a bit like the parcel in 'pass-the-parcel' — Walton is the first layer, Frankenstein is the second and the monster is wrapped up in the middle. It'd be quite a short game, come to think of it. And not the best prize.

The novel is structured using frame narratives

'in medias res' means 'in the middle of things'

1) A <u>frame narrative</u> is a story which contains another story within it, creating the effect of a 'story within a story'. Walton's letters frame Frankenstein's story, which in turn acts as a frame for the monster's account.

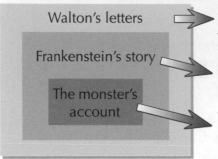

Walton's letters

Frankenstein's story

The monster's account

Shelley uses Walton's letters to <u>set the scene</u> and establish some <u>key themes</u> (see p.10) before Frankenstein's story begins. The letters start <u>in medias res</u>, which draws the reader straight into the action.

Frankenstein is the novel's <u>main narrator</u>. Shelley uses a <u>first-person</u> narrative so she can present Frankenstein's <u>motivations</u> and <u>feelings</u>.

The monster's account gives the reader his <u>perspective</u> on events. It encourages the reader to <u>sympathise</u> with him (see p.26).

2) By using this structure Shelley prompts her reader to question their <u>judgement</u> of characters and events. For example, Walton's letters present Frankenstein as a "wonderful man", but this is <u>challenged</u> by the events in Frankenstein's story, and by the monster's view of him as his "cursed creator!"

3) Walton's frame narrative also <u>emphasises</u> the novel's <u>warning</u> about the dangers of over-ambition. At the start, Walton is fully <u>committed</u> to his "great enterprise", but after hearing Frankenstein's story he's eventually persuaded to <u>abandon</u> his voyage. In this way, the novel is structured like a <u>moral lesson</u> for the reader.

Writer's Techniques

Frankenstein's and the monster's stories are <u>embedded narratives</u> — narratives that are included within other narratives. There are lots of <u>shorter</u> embedded narratives too, such as the <u>De Lacey family's history</u> (in Chapter 14) and <u>Elizabeth's letters</u>.

'Frankenstein' is an epistolary novel

1) An <u>epistolary</u> novel is a novel written in the form of <u>letters</u>. In *Frankenstein*, all of the narratives are <u>contained</u> within <u>Walton's letters</u> to his sister.

2) Shelley uses this form of novel for several reasons:

- It <u>engages</u> the reader with the story. Walton is writing to his sister, but it's as if he's directly <u>addressing</u> the reader.

- The opening letters add <u>intrigue</u>, because Walton only knows <u>part</u> of the story. For example, the "strange sight" of a "shape of a man" riding across the ice makes the reader want to find out more.

- It can make events seem more <u>dramatic</u>, because Walton writes about his <u>immediate</u> reactions to events — e.g. after his encounter with the monster, he writes "Great God! what a scene has just taken place!"

3) Other letters in the novel provide <u>insights</u> into more minor characters. For example, one of Elizabeth's letters provides the reader with <u>direct access</u> to her feelings about marriage — feelings that wouldn't otherwise be <u>included</u> in Frankenstein's first-person narrative.

© ulkan/iStockphoto.com

Structure, Narrative and Form

There are lots of parallels in the novel

© ITV/REX

1) Shelley encourages her reader to make <u>connections</u> and <u>comparisons</u> between different parts of the novel. For example:

- Frankenstein and the monster destroy one another's '<u>wives</u>'. This parallel emphasises the <u>vengeful</u> nature of their relationship, and the <u>similarities</u> between them (p.51).

- The De Laceys take in Safie and, similarly, the Frankensteins adopt Elizabeth. This creates a <u>pattern</u> of outsiders being <u>accepted</u> into families, which emphasises the monster's <u>exclusion</u>.

2) There are parallel <u>experiences</u> as well. For example, Justine and Frankenstein are both wrongly <u>imprisoned</u>, but whilst Justine is convicted, Frankenstein is set free.

Character — Frankenstein

Shelley may use this parallel to make the reader judge Frankenstein more <u>harshly</u>. He chooses not to <u>speak out</u> to save Justine, who's completely <u>innocent</u>, but later he himself is set free for a crime he's partly <u>responsible</u> for.

Frankenstein's hindsight provides hints about what will happen

1) Because Frankenstein's story is told with <u>hindsight</u>, he includes <u>hints</u> about later events. For example:

- Frankenstein constantly hints at his own <u>destruction</u>. Early in his narrative, his mother's death is "an omen" of his "future misery", and he says he was "destined" to suffer. This <u>foreshadowing</u> creates <u>suspense</u>, as the reader waits to find out <u>how</u> Frankenstein's story ended in despair.

- Frankenstein refers to Clerval as if he's <u>dead</u> — his "friendship <u>was</u>... devoted" — and says Clerval's "spirit" still visits him. This tells the reader that Clerval will <u>die</u> at some point in Frankenstein's narrative.

Foreshadowing is when a writer gives the reader clues about what will happen later on.

2) Using foreshadowing keeps the reader <u>engaged</u>, because they want to find out exactly what happens.

The narrative encourages the reader to make judgements

1) Shelley <u>doesn't</u> use an <u>omniscient</u> narrator — instead, she uses three narrators who each have their own opinion of events. This means that the reader has to make their <u>own judgements</u> about the characters' actions.

An omniscient narrator is a narrator who knows everything that's going on in the story.

2) Shelley also uses an <u>open ending</u> to make the reader think about the novel's <u>message</u> and <u>themes</u>. For example, it's unknown if Walton will ever return to the Arctic, so it's up to the reader to <u>decide</u> whether he's truly listened to Frankenstein's warning about the dangers of <u>over-ambition</u>.

Write about why Shelley uses these types of narrative...

Sadly, writing 'it's a frame narrative' or 'there's no omniscient narrator' isn't enough to get you top marks — you need to write about <u>why</u> Shelley uses these techniques. These pages should give you some ideas.

Symbolism

There are some pretty common symbols used in *Frankenstein* — things like light and dark, for example. But it's not quite as simple as light = good stuff and dark = bad. Shelley was way more inventive than that...

Light symbolises new knowledge and its dangers

1) Both Frankenstein and Walton use <u>light</u> to describe the <u>new</u> knowledge they seek. Walton wants to discover things in the Arctic that will help mankind, so he <u>optimistically</u> imagines it as a "country of eternal light". Similarly, when Frankenstein discovered how to create life from death a "sudden light broke in" upon him. Their symbolism suggests that new knowledge can <u>illuminate</u> and <u>benefit</u> mankind.

2) However, Shelley also uses light to symbolise the <u>dangers</u> that new knowledge can bring. A <u>lightning</u> strike shows Frankenstein the <u>power</u> of electricity, but a tree is "<u>shattered</u>" and "utterly <u>destroyed</u>" by it. This symbolises the danger of pursuing some types of knowledge (see p.37), and its <u>destruction</u> of Frankenstein.

> Light is also used to symbolise <u>creation</u>. Frankenstein animates the monster with a "<u>spark</u> <u>of being</u>". However, like the lightning strike, this "spark" will also result in <u>destruction</u>.

Shelley uses fire to symbolise different things

Fire imagery also links to the Prometheus myth (see p.8).

1) The monster is "<u>overcome with delight</u>" when he discovers fire, since it provides light and warmth, but he <u>hurts</u> himself on the "live embers". Here, Shelley uses fire as a symbol for <u>knowledge</u> because, like fire, knowledge both <u>benefits</u> and <u>harms</u> the monster.

2) Fire is also associated with <u>evil</u>. The monster <u>destroys</u> the De Laceys' cottage with "forked and destroying tongues" of fire, which is a physical representation of his "<u>hellish rage</u>".

© SNAP/REX

> **Background and Context**
>
> These descriptions also link the monster with <u>Satan</u> in *Paradise Lost*, who's banished by God to a "<u>lake of fire</u>" (<u>Hell</u>). Also, Satan transforms into a snake with a <u>forked tongue</u> when he tempts Adam and Eve.

3) At the end of the novel, the monster plans to <u>die</u> in "<u>torturing flames</u>", suggesting that fire symbolises <u>ultimate destruction</u>.

Darkness symbolises the mysterious and disturbing

1) Frankenstein's <u>experiments</u> are conducted in <u>darkness</u> — he calls them his "midnight labours", and the monster is brought to life on a "dreary night". This makes his work seem <u>mysterious</u> and <u>sinister</u>.

2) Before he creates the monster, Frankenstein says that "Darkness had <u>no effect</u>" upon him, but afterwards, darkness begins to symbolise his <u>mental anguish</u>.

3) He feels "a darkness" around him after Clerval's death, and after his marriage he's "calm during the day", but feels "a thousand fears" at night. This emphasises how his <u>unnatural</u> creation has left him permanently <u>disturbed</u>.

KEY QUOTE

"I saw around me... a dense and frightful darkness"

To begin with, night and darkness don't bother Frankenstein, and he's happy to hang out with dead bodies. Towards the end of the novel, his nights are plagued by nightmares and disturbing visions. Not so ideal.

Imagery

Imagery is language that creates a picture in the reader's mind. Right now, I'm picturing a roast dinner and a steaming hot apple crumble with homemade custard. Sadly, Shelley's imagery isn't always that comforting.

There's a lot of biblical imagery in 'Frankenstein'

1) Shelley uses biblical imagery to explore ideas about good and evil:

Images of good	Images of evil
Women are often associated with heavenly imagery. Elizabeth is described as "a being heaven-sent", emphasising her goodness.	Frankenstein and the monster both talk of carrying a "hell within" them. This associates them with evil.
Caroline Frankenstein is a "guardian angel" to the poor, emphasising her selflessness.	The monster says he's a "fallen angel", suggesting that he's turned from good to evil.
The monster calls Frankenstein his "natural lord and king", suggesting that he's a God-like creator and associating him with goodness.	Frankenstein is also linked to Satan — he says he's punished for imitating God, "like the archangel who aspired to omnipotence".

2) Biblical imagery would have been very familiar to Shelley's original readers, so she uses it to emphasise qualities about her characters.

Background and Context

Using biblical imagery also links the novel more strongly to *Paradise Lost* — see p.8.

Shelley uses imagery of nature's power

1) Frankenstein uses natural imagery to describe his passion for science — he says it was "like a mountain river" that became a "torrent" which ruined his dreams. Here, he presents himself as a passive victim, carried along by powerful forces he can't control, as if he's blameless for his actions.

2) When Frankenstein is fifteen, he watches a thunderstorm of "dazzling light" and "frightful loudness". Shelley emphasises nature's power by using imagery that appeals to the reader's sense of sight and sound.

3) Imagery of extreme weather is also used to create tension. Before Frankenstein sees the figure of the monster, there's a storm described as a "noble war in the sky". This imagery of violent nature makes the monster's appearance more dramatic.

For more on nature's role in the novel, see p.50.

Writer's Techniques

Extreme weather is a common feature of Gothic novels — see p.51.

© Moviestore Collection/REX

EXAM TIP

Comment on what imagery tells you about a character...

Describing your passion as a "mountain river" can seem a tad melodramatic — but that's kind of the point. The way Frankenstein uses nature's power to describe his emotions shows how intensely he feels things.

Setting

To be honest, the settings in this novel are pretty bleak, but I guess that fits with the general doom and gloom.

Much of the novel is set in cold and wild places

Extremes are a feature of Gothic novels — see the next page.

1) *Frankenstein* is mostly set in <u>wild</u> and <u>cold</u> places, such as the Alps, the Arctic seas and a remote island in the Orkneys. These settings emphasise the <u>isolation</u> of characters like Frankenstein and Walton.

Character — The Monster

The monster is <u>suited</u> to wild landscapes. He's able to bear "the extremes of heat and cold" better than Frankenstein. This makes him seem <u>stronger</u>, but also <u>less human</u>.

2) These settings also emphasise the <u>extremes</u> to which the characters are pushed. Frankenstein's and Walton's ambitions lead them to the <u>remotest</u> locations possible, and Frankenstein pushes himself beyond what his body can cope with — he suffers "<u>infinite fatigue</u>", and eventually dies.

3) Shelley uses setting to highlight the <u>danger</u> of Walton's ambition to reach the North Pole. He and his crew become "<u>surrounded</u> by mountains of ice which <u>admit of no escape</u> and <u>threaten</u> every moment to <u>crush</u>" their ship. It's as if nature is actively trying to <u>stop</u> Walton's expedition.

Settings often reflect Frankenstein's emotions

1) The Scottish <u>island</u> where Frankenstein makes the female monster is "desolate and appalling". This reflects his <u>bleak emotions</u> and his <u>isolation</u>.

2) Similarly, the monster is created on a "<u>dreary</u> night", when the "rain pattered <u>dismally</u> against the panes" — this mirrors Frankenstein's "<u>anxiety</u>".

3) The morning after, Frankenstein describes the sky as "black and comfortless", reflecting his <u>hopeless</u> mood.

Writer's Techniques

Describing the sky as "<u>comfortless</u>" is an example of <u>pathetic fallacy</u>, where a writer uses human emotions to describe objects or aspects of nature.

© SNAP/REX

Settings are a good way to create mood. Shelley's bleak settings create a sense of unease and foreboding.

Natural settings can comfort and restore characters

1) Frankenstein feels that "wonderful and stupendous" <u>views</u> of nature can help him to <u>forget</u> "the passing cares of life". This is a '<u>Romantic</u>' view of the natural world.

Background and Context

For 'Romantic' writers, nature is a <u>powerful force</u> that inspires <u>intense emotions</u> and <u>restores</u> people in times of despair or sadness (see p.7).

2) The monster is comforted by nature too. His senses are "<u>gratified</u> and <u>refreshed</u>" by beautiful sights, making him seem more <u>human</u>.

Character — Frankenstein

Frankenstein <u>isn't always</u> restored by nature. When he travels in Europe, he feels he's "shut up every avenue to enjoyment", <u>despite</u> the beautiful scenery around him. This suggests that his <u>unnatural</u> work has <u>damaged</u> his appreciation of nature.

3) <u>Clerval</u> is particularly affected by the "beauties" of nature, which make him "<u>enjoy existence</u>".

EXAM TIP

Write about how setting is linked to emotion...

In your exam, you could mention that natural settings inspire intense emotions in several characters. For example, Clerval feels he's been "transported to fairy-land" as soon as he sees a nice glacier or a pretty tree.

The Gothic Novel

The Gothic novel is a specific genre of fiction which contains elements of horror and mystery. Other Gothic novels include Robert Louis Stevenson's *The Strange Case of Dr Jekyll and Mr Hyde* and Bram Stoker's *Dracula*.

'Frankenstein' is a Gothic novel

Gothic novels often deal with <u>disturbing</u> events and <u>extreme</u> situations:

Disturbing settings	Frankenstein visits <u>graveyards</u>, <u>slaughter houses</u> and <u>dissecting rooms</u> to study the "corruption of death", and makes the monster in his "workshop of filthy creation".
Troubling secrets	Frankenstein can't bring himself to tell anyone about his "<u>secret toil</u>", even when Justine is sentenced to death. He carries with him a "<u>burden</u>" of "<u>mysterious woe</u>".
The supernatural	Frankenstein tells Walton to "Prepare to hear of occurrences which are usually deemed <u>marvellous</u>". His creation is often called a "<u>monster</u>" or a "<u>fiend</u>".
Dreams and visions	After he creates the monster, Frankenstein has a <u>dream</u> in which Elizabeth transforms into the "<u>corpse</u>" of his dead mother, with "<u>grave-worms crawling</u>" in her clothes.
Madness	Frankenstein initially says he wasn't a "madman" to think of creating life, but later he calls his work a "<u>mad enthusiasm</u>", and frequently suffers from a "<u>nervous fever</u>".
Extremes	All three narrators use <u>hyperbole</u> (see p.52). The novel also features extreme <u>weather</u>, <u>emotions</u> and <u>settings</u> that push some characters to their <u>limits</u> (see p.50).

Frankenstein and the monster are Gothic doubles

1) The <u>double</u> (or <u>doppelgänger</u>) is a key <u>feature</u> of Gothic novels. Frankenstein and his monster are doubles of one another.

2) There are many similarities in their <u>personalities</u>. They both have an "ardent" desire to acquire <u>knowledge</u>, but it <u>harms</u> both of them. They're both <u>intelligent</u>, <u>isolated</u> and become <u>obsessed</u> with revenge.

3) Each character feels that he's a <u>version</u> of the other. The monster says to Frankenstein, "my form is a filthy type of yours", and Frankenstein sees the monster as "my own spirit let loose from the grave". This Gothic doubling suggests that the monster is the <u>unnatural</u>, <u>darker side</u> of Frankenstein.

4) Towards the <u>end</u> of the novel, Frankenstein believes that other people will "abhor" him and "hunt" him from the world, <u>mirroring</u> the monster's earlier suffering, and by the time he meets Walton, he "gnashes his teeth". Shelley suggests that Frankenstein has <u>become</u> like the monster he created.

> <u>Walton</u> and <u>Clerval</u> can also be read as doubles for Frankenstein — they both have qualities in common with him (see p.28 and 29).

"Memory brought madness... a real insanity possessed me"

Frankenstein has become one of the most famous examples of Gothic fiction — make sure you can pick out the key features of the Gothic genre in the novel and comment on the effect they have on the reader.

Language

The monster "ardently" desires to learn language, and examiners ardently desire to read about it. Once you've read this page, try jotting down the names of some language features, with examples from the novel.

All three narrators use a lot of similes and metaphors

1) A common feature of Frankenstein's language is the way he describes his <u>emotions</u> as if they're <u>physical things</u>. His feelings are "like a hurricane" and his vengeance is "like a mighty tide". These <u>similes</u> use the <u>power</u> of nature (see p.49) to emphasise Frankenstein's <u>intense</u> emotions.

2) Walton uses a <u>metaphor</u> to describe Frankenstein, saying he's a "<u>gallant vessel</u>" that's been "<u>wrecked</u>" by a storm, which emphasises how Frankenstein's experiences have <u>damaged</u> him. Walton's language could also suggest that he's <u>worried</u> about the dangers facing his own ship.

3) The monster uses a <u>simile</u> to describe Safie's singing — he says it's "like a nightingale of the woods". This emphasises the <u>purity</u> of her voice, and also demonstrates his <u>admiration</u> for <u>nature</u>.

> **Background and Context**
>
> Frankenstein and the monster often <u>compare</u> themselves to characters from *Paradise Lost*. Shelley uses these comparisons to explore ideas of good and evil (see p.8).

There are a lot of exaggerated descriptions

1) All three narrators use <u>exaggerated language</u> — for example, Frankenstein says he loves Clerval with an affection that "knew <u>no bounds</u>".

2) Shelley uses some specific <u>types</u> of exaggerated language:

- <u>superlatives</u> — Frankenstein describes Elizabeth as "the <u>purest</u> creature on earth", and Walton feels "the <u>most</u> poignant grief". *Superlatives refer to the most or least of something.*

- <u>exclamations</u> — Frankenstein cries "save me! Save me!" to Clerval and the monster condemns his "Cursed, cursed creator!"

3) Exaggerated language shows that all three characters <u>lack moderation</u> and <u>self-control</u>. This makes them seem <u>unpredictable</u> and dangerous. *Exaggerated language is also called <u>hyperbole</u>.*

© Moviestore Collection/REX

The monster's language is eloquent

1) The monster becomes particularly "<u>eloquent and persuasive</u>". He uses <u>rhetorical questions</u> (e.g. "tell me why I should pity man more than he pities me?") and the <u>power of three</u> (e.g. "wretched, helpless, and alone") to make his arguments sound more <u>persuasive</u>.

2) His words have the "<u>power</u>" to move people, and both Frankenstein and Walton feel the "<u>strange effect</u>" of his speeches. However, his words aren't enough, and people are still <u>prejudiced</u> against him.

> **Theme — Prejudice**
>
> When the monster <u>covers</u> Frankenstein's eyes, it's because he wants him to "<u>hear</u>" and not <u>see</u>. He knows that people are prejudiced against his appearance, and <u>persuasive language</u> is his <u>only hope</u> of getting people to <u>accept</u> him.

"hear me before you give vent to your hatred"

When you're writing about the effects of Shelley's language, it helps to use the proper terminology — words like 'metaphor' and 'superlative'. That'll make it crystal clear to the examiner that you know your stuff.

Practice Questions

Aha, the final set of quick questions. These will check that you've got a basic understanding of Shelley's clever techniques. Make sure you can complete them all before you move onto page 54.

Quick Questions

1) What is a frame narrative?

2) Give one example of an embedded narrative in *Frankenstein*.

3) What is an epistolary novel?

4) What does 'foreshadowing' mean?

5) Give one way in which Shelley encourages the reader to make their own judgements.

6) Find a quote from the novel where light is used to symbolise new knowledge.

7) a) Find an example in the novel where biblical imagery associates a character with good.
   b) Find an example in the novel where biblical imagery associates a character with evil.

8) Write down two adjectives to describe how each of these settings are presented in the novel:
   a) the Arctic seas   b) the Orkney islands

9) Give two ways in which Frankenstein and the monster are Gothic doubles (or doppelgängers).

10) a) Other than the double, name one other feature of Gothic novels.
    b) Give an example of this feature in *Frankenstein*.

11) Find a quote that demonstrates Frankenstein's use of exaggerated language.

12) Which character's language is described as "eloquent and persuasive"?

Practice Questions

It's time to unlock your inner Victor and think some deep thoughts. Write your answers using the P.E.E.D. structure (it's explained on p.60) — that means you need to find some quotes and evidence to support what you write.

In-depth Questions

1) Write a paragraph explaining why you think Shelley structures the novel using frame narratives.

2) Explain two effects of the epistolary form in *Frankenstein*.

3) What hints are there in Frankenstein's narrative that his story will end badly?

4) Explain how darkness is used to symbolise the mysterious and disturbing in *Frankenstein*. Use quotes from the text to support your answer.

5) How does Shelley use biblical imagery to contribute to her characterisation in *Frankenstein*? Mention at least two characters in your answer.

6) How does Shelley use setting to show Frankenstein's emotions?

7) Briefly explain why you think Shelley presents Frankenstein and the monster as Gothic doubles.

8) What does the exaggerated language used by Walton, Frankenstein and the monster tell us about their characters? Use quotes from the text to support your answer.

9) *"Language is the most valuable piece of knowledge the monster acquires."* How far do you agree with this statement?

Practice Questions

Exam-style questions are one of the best ways to prepare for the real deal, so give some of these a go. See if you can do a few under time pressure as well. Make sure you plan your answers first — we've seen what happens when you launch into something without thinking about the consequences, and it ain't pretty. There's some handy advice on planning (and all the other bits of essay writing) in Section Six.

Exam-style Questions

1) Using the extract below as a starting point, describe the narrative structure of *Frankenstein* and explain its effect on the reader.

Taken from Letter IV

My affection for my guest increases every day. He excites at once my admiration and my pity to an astonishing degree. How can I see so noble a creature destroyed by misery without feeling the most poignant grief? He is so gentle, yet so wise; his mind is so cultivated, and when he speaks, although his words are culled with the choicest art, yet they flow with rapidity and unparalleled eloquence.

He is now much recovered from his illness and is continually on the deck, apparently watching for the sledge that preceded his own. Yet, although unhappy, he is not so utterly occupied by his own misery but that he interests himself deeply in the projects of others. He has frequently conversed with me on mine, which I have communicated to him without disguise. He entered attentively into all my arguments in favour of my eventual success, and into every minute detail of the measures I had taken to secure it. I was easily led by the sympathy which he evinced to use the language of my heart, to give utterance to the burning ardour of my soul, and to say, with all the fervour that warmed me, how gladly I would sacrifice my fortune, my existence, my every hope to the furtherance of my enterprise. One man's life or death were but a small price to pay for the acquirement of the knowledge which I sought, for the dominion I should acquire and transmit over the elemental foes of our race. As I spoke, a dark gloom spread over my listener's countenance. At first I perceived that he tried to suppress his emotion: he placed his hands before his eyes, and my voice quivered and failed me as I beheld tears trickle fast from between his fingers; a groan burst from his heaving breast. I paused; at length he spoke, in broken accents: "Unhappy man! Do you share my madness? Have you drunk also of the intoxicating draught? Hear me; let me reveal my tale, and you will dash the cup from your lips!"

---

2) "The natural world in *Frankenstein* is presented as more of a friend than a foe."
How far do you agree with this statement?

3) *"Three years before, I was engaged in the same manner and had created a fiend whose unparalleled barbarity had desolated my heart and filled it forever with the bitterest remorse."* (Victor Frankenstein)

Using this quote as a starting point, explore Shelley's use of language in the novel.

Exam Preparation

Getting to know the text will put you at a massive advantage in the exam. It's not enough just to read it though — you've got to get to grips with the nitty-gritty bits. It's all about gathering evidence...

The exam questions will test four main skills

You will need to show the examiner that you can:

1) Write about the text in a <u>thoughtful way</u> — <u>picking out</u> appropriate <u>examples</u> and <u>quotations</u> to back up your opinions.

2) <u>Identify</u> and <u>explain</u> features of the text's <u>form</u>, <u>structure</u> and <u>language</u>. Show how the author uses these to create <u>meanings</u> and <u>effects</u>.

3) Relate the text to its <u>cultural, social and historical background</u>.

4) Write in a <u>clear</u>, <u>well-structured</u> way. <u>5%</u> of the marks in your English Literature exams are for <u>spelling</u>, <u>punctuation</u> and <u>grammar</u>. Make sure that your writing is as <u>accurate</u> as possible.

Preparation is important

1) It's <u>important</u> to cover <u>all</u> the <u>different sections</u> of this book in your <u>revision</u>. You need to make sure you <u>understand</u> the text's <u>context</u>, <u>plot</u>, <u>characters</u>, <u>themes</u> and <u>writer's techniques</u>.

2) In the <u>exam</u>, you'll need to <u>bring together</u> your <u>ideas</u> about these topics to answer the question <u>quickly</u>.

3) Think about the different <u>characters</u> and <u>themes</u> in the text, and write down some <u>key points</u> and <u>ideas</u> about each one. Then, find some <u>evidence</u> to support each point — this could be something from <u>any</u> of the <u>sections</u> in this book. You could set out your evidence in a <u>table</u> like this:

Theme: Family	
Supportive	Frankenstein's family support him, e.g. his father travels to Ireland. The De Laceys make sacrifices for each other.
Welcoming	The Frankensteins and the De Laceys welcome new people into their families (Elizabeth, Justine, Safie).
Motherhood	Elizabeth and Justine act as mothers to William. Justine's mother is a "strange perversity" for not loving her child.
The monster	A contrast to the happy families in the novel — has no family, and is rejected by Frankenstein and the De Laceys.
Frankenstein as a parent	Frankenstein doesn't take any parental responsibility. His neglect affects the monster's personality and actions.

Preparing to succeed — a cunning plot indeed...

Knowing the plot inside out will be unbelievably helpful in the exam. It'll help you to stay calm and make sure you write a brilliant answer that positively glitters with little gems of evidence. The exam's just a chance for you to show off...

The Exam Question

This page deals with how to approach an exam question. The stuff below will help you get started on a scorching exam answer, more scorching than, say, a phoenix cooking fiery fajitas in a flaming furnace.

Read the question carefully and underline key words

1) The style of question you'll get depends on which <u>exam board</u> you're taking.

2) Read all the <u>instructions</u> carefully. Make sure you know <u>how many</u> questions you need to answer and <u>how much time</u> you should spend answering each one.

3) If the question has <u>more than one part</u>, look at the total number of marks for each bit. This should help you to plan your <u>time</u> in the exam.

4) <u>Read</u> the question at least <u>twice</u> so you completely understand it. <u>Underline</u> the key words. If you're given an <u>extract</u>, underline <u>important</u> words or phrases in that too.

Henry didn't read the weather report carefully enough when planning his weekend activities.

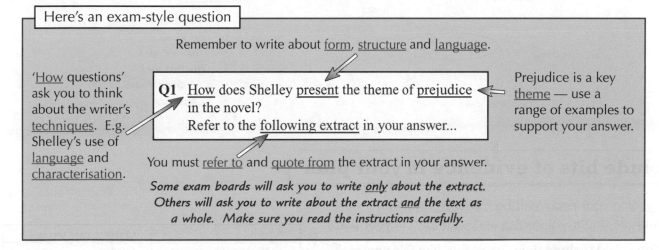

Here's an exam-style question

Remember to write about <u>form</u>, <u>structure</u> and <u>language</u>.

'<u>How</u> questions' ask you to think about the writer's <u>techniques</u>. E.g. Shelley's use of <u>language</u> and <u>characterisation</u>.

Q1 <u>How</u> does Shelley <u>present</u> the theme of <u>prejudice</u> in the novel?
Refer to the <u>following extract</u> in your answer...

Prejudice is a key <u>theme</u> — use a range of examples to support your answer.

You must <u>refer to</u> and <u>quote from</u> the extract in your answer.

Some exam boards will ask you to write <u>only</u> about the extract. Others will ask you to write about the extract <u>and</u> the text as a whole. Make sure you read the instructions carefully.

Get to know exam language

Some <u>words</u> come up time and again in <u>exam questions</u>. Have a look at some <u>specimen</u> questions, pick out words that are <u>often used</u> in questions and make sure that you <u>understand</u> what they mean. You could <u>write a few down</u> whilst you're revising. For example:

Question Word	You need to...
Explore / Explain	Show <u>how</u> the writer deals with a <u>theme</u>, <u>character</u> or <u>idea</u>. Make several <u>different</u> points to answer the question.
How does	Think about the <u>techniques</u> or <u>literary features</u> that the author uses to get their point across.
Give examples	Use <u>direct quotes</u> and describe <u>events</u> from the text in your own words.
Refer to	Read the question so that you know if you need to write about just an <u>extract</u>, or an extract and the <u>rest of the text</u>.

The advice squad — the best cops in the NYPD...

Whatever question you're asked in the exam, your answer should touch on the main characters, themes, structure and language of the text. All the stuff we've covered in the rest of the book in fact. It's so neat, it's almost like we planned it.

Planning Your Answer

I'll say this once — and then I'll probably repeat it several times — it is absolutely, completely, totally and utterly essential that you make a plan before you start writing. Only a fool jumps right in without a plan...

Plan your answer before you start

1) If you plan, you're less likely to forget something <u>important</u>.

2) A good plan will help you <u>organise</u> your ideas — and write a good, <u>well-structured</u> essay.

3) Write your plan at the <u>top of your answer booklet</u> and draw a <u>neat line</u> through it when you've finished.

4) <u>Don't</u> spend <u>too long</u> on your plan. It's only <u>rough work</u>, so you don't need to write in full sentences. Here are a few <u>examples</u> of different ways you can plan your answer:

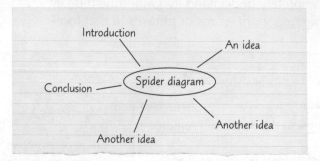

Bullet points...

- Introduction...
- An idea...
- The next idea...
- Another idea...
- Yet another idea...
- Conclusion...

Include bits of evidence in your plan

1) <u>Writing</u> your essay will be much <u>easier</u> if you include <u>important quotes</u> and <u>examples</u> in your plan.

2) You could include them in a <u>table</u> like this one:

A point...	Quote to back this up...
Another point...	Quote...
A different point...	Example...
A brand new point...	Quote...

3) <u>Don't</u> spend <u>too long</u> writing out quotes though. It's just to make sure you <u>don't forget</u> anything when you write your answer.

Structure your answer

Introduction
↓
Middle Section
— paragraphs
expanding
your
argument.
↓
Conclusion

1) Your <u>introduction</u> should give a brief answer to the question you're writing about. Make it clear how you're going to <u>tackle the topic</u>.

2) The <u>middle section</u> of your essay should explain your answer in detail and give evidence to back it up. Write a <u>paragraph</u> for each point you make. Make sure you <u>comment</u> on your evidence and <u>explain how</u> it helps to <u>prove</u> your point.

3) Remember to write a <u>conclusion</u> — a paragraph at the end which <u>sums up</u> your <u>main points</u>. There's <u>more</u> about introductions and conclusions on the <u>next page</u>.

Dirk finally felt ready to tackle the topic.

To plan or not to plan, that is the question...

The answer is yes, yes, a thousand times yes. Often students dive right in, worried that planning will take up valuable time. But 5 minutes spent organising a well-structured answer is loads better than pages of waffle. Mmm waffles.

Section Six — Exam Advice

Writing Introductions and Conclusions

Now you've made that plan that I was banging on about on the last page, you'll know what your main points are. This is going to make writing your introduction and conclusion as easy as pie.

Get to the point straight away in your introduction

1) First, you need to <u>work out</u> what the question is <u>asking you</u> to do:

> How is the character of Clerval important to the novel?

> The question is <u>asking you</u> to think about the <u>role</u> of <u>Clerval</u> in the text.
> Plan your essay by thinking about <u>how</u> this character <u>links</u> to the text's overall <u>message</u>.

2) When you've <u>planned</u> your essay, you should <u>begin</u> by giving a <u>clear answer</u> to the <u>question</u> in a sentence or two. Use the <u>rest</u> of the <u>introduction</u> to <u>develop</u> this idea. Try to include the <u>main paragraph ideas</u> that you have listed in your plan, but <u>save</u> the <u>evidence</u> for later.

3) You could also use the <u>introduction</u> to give your <u>opinion</u>. Whatever you do, make sure your introduction makes it <u>clear</u> how your answer <u>fits the question</u>.

Your conclusion must answer the question

1) The <u>most important</u> thing you have to do at the <u>end</u> of your writing is to <u>summarise</u> your <u>answer</u> to the question.

2) It's your <u>last chance</u> to persuade the examiner, so make your <u>main point</u> again.

3) Use your <u>last sentence</u> to really <u>impress</u> the <u>examiner</u> — it will make your essay <u>stand out</u>. You could <u>develop</u> your own <u>opinion</u> of the text or <u>highlight</u> which of your <u>points</u> you thought was the most <u>interesting</u>.

The examiner was struggling to see the answer clearly.

Use the question words in your introduction and conclusion

1) Try to use <u>words</u> or <u>phrases</u> from the <u>question</u> in your introduction and conclusion.

> How does Shelley use setting in the novel?

2) This will show the examiner that you're <u>answering the question</u>.

> Shelley uses setting in 'Frankenstein' to create symbolic meaning. The settings link to the main themes of the novel, such as isolation and ambition.

The first line of the introduction gives a clear answer, which will lead on to the rest of the essay.

3) This will also help you keep the question <u>fresh in your mind</u> so your answer doesn't <u>wander off-topic</u>.

I've come to the conclusion that I really like pie...

To conclude, the introduction eases the examiner in gently, whilst the conclusion is your last chance to impress.
But remember — the examiner doesn't want to see any new points lurking in those closing sentences.

Writing Main Paragraphs

So we've covered the beginning and the end, now it's time for the meaty bit. The roast beef in between the prawn cocktail and the treacle tart. This page is about how to structure your paragraphs. It's quite simple...

P.E.E.D. is how to put your argument together

Remember to start a new paragraph every time you make a new point.

1) P.E.E.D. stands for: Point, Example, Explain, Develop.

2) Begin each paragraph by making a point. Then give an example from the text (either a quote or a description). Next, explain how your example backs up your point.

3) Finally, try to develop your point by writing about its effect on the reader, how it links to another part of the text or what the writer's intention is in including it.

Use short quotes to support your ideas

1) Don't just write out long chunks of the text to explain things...

> The monster is physically large. He is "a being which had the shape of a man, but apparently of gigantic stature".

This just gives an example from the text without offering any explanation or analysis.

2) Instead, it's much better to use short quotes as evidence to support a point you're making.

3) It makes the essay structure clearer and smoother if most quotes are embedded in your sentences.

It's better to use short, embedded quotes as evidence. Then you can go on to explain them.

> The monster is described as being "gigantic" by Walton, which shows that he is physically intimidating to others. This helps the reader to understand why people are so afraid of his appearance.

Get to know some literary language

1) Using literary terms in your answer will make your essay stand out — as long as you use them correctly.

2) When you're revising, think about literary terms that are relevant to the text and how you might include them in an essay. Take a look at the table below for some examples.

Literary Term	Definition	Example
Simile	Compares one thing to another, often using 'like' and 'as'.	"The saintly soul of Elizabeth shone like a shrine-dedicated lamp"
Intertextuality	Linking to another text in order to suggest an idea to the reader.	"I ought to be thy Adam, but I am rather the fallen angel"
Metaphor	Describing something by saying it is something else.	"I am a blasted tree"

This page is so exciting — I nearly...

Now now, let's all be grown-ups and avoid the obvious joke. It's a good way of remembering how to structure your paragraphs though. Point, Example, Explain, Develop. Simple. Maybe we could make a rap or something... anyone?

In the Exam

Keeping cool in the exam can be tricky. But if you take in all the stuff on this page, you'll soon have it down to a fine art. Then you can stroll out of that exam hall with the swagger of an essay-writing master.

Don't panic if you make a mistake

1) Okay, so say you've timed the exam beautifully. Instead of putting your feet up on the desk for the last 5 minutes, it's a good idea to <u>read through</u> your <u>answers</u> and <u>correct any mistakes</u>...

2) If you want to get rid of a mistake, <u>cross it out</u>. <u>Don't scribble</u> it out as this can look messy. Make any corrections <u>neatly</u> and <u>clearly</u> instead of writing on top of the words you've already written.

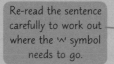

techniques
The author uses various literary ~~teknikues~~ to explore this theme .

This is the clearest way to correct a mistake. Don't be tempted to try writing on top of the original word.

3) If you've <u>left out</u> a <u>word</u> or a <u>phrase</u> and you've got space to add it in <u>above</u> the line it's missing from, write the missing bit above the line with a '∧' to show exactly where it should go.

Re-read the sentence carefully to work out where the '∧' symbol needs to go.

and hyperbole
The writer uses imagery to draw attention to this point.

4) If you've left out whole <u>sentences</u> or <u>paragraphs</u>, write them in a <u>separate section</u> at the <u>end</u> of the essay. Put a <u>star</u> (*) next to both the <u>extra writing</u> and the <u>place</u> you want it to go.

Always keep an eye on the time

1) It's surprisingly <u>easy</u> to <u>run out of time</u> in exams. You've got to leave <u>enough time</u> to answer <u>all</u> the questions you're asked to do. You've also got to leave enough time to <u>finish</u> each essay properly — with a <u>clear ending</u>.

2) Here are some <u>tips</u> on how to <u>avoid</u> running out of time:

- Work out <u>how much time</u> you have for each part of your answer <u>before</u> you <u>start</u>.

- Take off a few minutes at the beginning to <u>plan</u>, and a <u>few minutes</u> at the end for your <u>conclusion</u>.

- Make sure you have a <u>watch</u> to <u>time yourself</u> — and keep checking it.

- Be <u>strict</u> with yourself — if you spend <u>too long</u> on one part of your answer, you may run out of time.

- If you're <u>running out of time</u>, keep <u>calm</u>, <u>finish</u> the <u>point</u> you're on and move on to your <u>conclusion</u>.

Stephanie never had a problem with keeping cool.

Treat an exam like a spa day — just relax...

Some people actually do lose the plot when they get into the exam. The trick is to keep calm and well... carry on. If you make sure you get your exam technique sorted, you'll be as relaxed as a sloth in a room full of easy chairs.

Sample Exam Question

And now the bit you've all been waiting for — a sample exam question and a lovely little plan.
Go and make yourself a cup of tea, then settle down and enjoy.

Here's a sample exam question...

Read this feisty exam question. That's the best way to start...

In the exam, you'll be given the full extract in the exam paper.

Read the question carefully. Underline the important bits.

Write about context — how the time in which Shelley was writing might influence her view of ambition.

Q1 In Chapter Four, read the section that begins with "No-one can conceive the variety of feelings..." and ends "... lost all soul or sensation but for this one pursuit."

Beginning with this passage, write about how Shelley presents ambition as dangerous in the novel.

You'll need to discuss the passage given in detail but you also need to refer to the rest of the book.

You need to think about what it is that makes ambition dangerous. E.g. the way it's presented, its effects, the language used to describe it.

Think about how Shelley uses language and setting to present the theme of ambition.

Here's how you could plan your answer

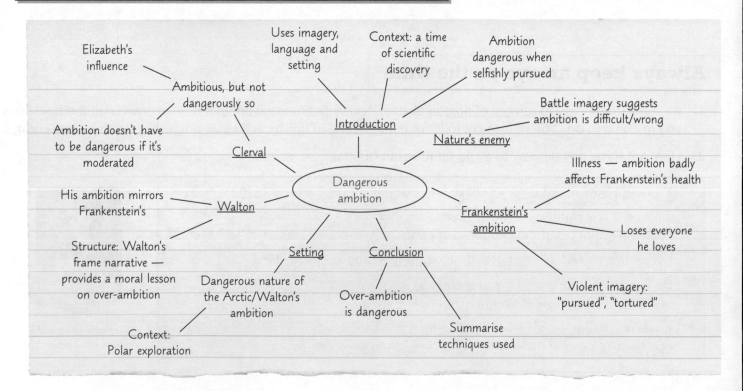

Elizabeth's influence

Ambitious, but not dangerously so

Ambition doesn't have to be dangerous if it's moderated

His ambition mirrors Frankenstein's

Structure: Walton's frame narrative — provides a moral lesson on over-ambition

Context: Polar exploration

Clerval

Walton

Setting

Dangerous nature of the Arctic/Walton's ambition

Uses imagery, language and setting

Context: a time of scientific discovery

Ambition dangerous when selfishly pursued

Introduction

Nature's enemy

Battle imagery suggests ambition is difficult/wrong

Illness — ambition badly affects Frankenstein's health

Dangerous ambition

Frankenstein's ambition

Loses everyone he loves

Conclusion

Over-ambition is dangerous

Summarise techniques used

Violent imagery: "pursued", "tortured"

What do examiners eat? Why, egg-sam-wiches of course...

The most important thing to remember is DON'T PANIC. Take a deep breath, read the question, read it again, write a plan... take another deep breath... and start writing. Leave a few minutes at the end to check your answer too.

Worked Answer

These pages will show you how to take an OK answer and turn it into a really good one that will impress the examiner.

Use your introduction to get off to a good start

These pages are all about how to word your sentences to impress the examiner, so we haven't included everything from the plan on page 62.

You might start with something like...

> Shelley presents the dangers of ambition through the characters of Frankenstein and Walton, and by using a variety of techniques, such as imagery and setting.

1) This intro is okay. It acknowledges that Shelley explores the dangers of ambition in different ways.
2) It's also a good idea to use the key words in the question to give your essay focus and show the examiner you're on track and that you're thinking about the question from the start.
3) But there's still room for improvement...

> In 'Frankenstein', Shelley presents ambition as dangerous by using a variety of techniques, such as imagery, language and setting, and especially through the characters of Frankenstein and Walton. In writing 'Frankenstein', Shelley took inspiration from things she had read or heard about. Scientists at the time were ambitiously trying to discover secrets about the origins of life, and explorers were seeking glory by trying to find passages through the Arctic seas. With this in mind, Shelley uses Frankenstein and Walton (a scientist and an explorer) to warn of the dangers of ambition when it is obsessively pursued.

This tells the examiner what the essay's about and shows that you've thought about your essay structure.

This intro talks about the social and historical context.

Develop each point with detailed comments and quotes

> Shelley suggests that it is unhealthy to obsessively pursue ambition by showing the effect that it has on Frankenstein, who becomes ill and loses weight while he is creating the monster.

1) This paragraph makes a point about the extract, and gives some detail about what happens in the scene. But it doesn't develop the point, and it doesn't give any quotes as evidence.
2) You should develop your points with evidence and analysis:

> When Frankenstein is making the monster, Shelley presents the idea that obsessively pursuing ambition is dangerous and unhealthy. Shelley uses violent imagery to emphasise the dangerous nature of Frankenstein's work — he "pursued nature" and "tortured" animals. This imagery encourages the reader to view Frankenstein's work as something disturbing and dangerous. Frankenstein's unhealthy work also makes him physically unwell — he works so hard on the monster that he becomes "pale" and "emaciated". Shelley's use of the extreme word "emaciated" suggests that Frankenstein has endangered his physical health by obsessively pursuing ambition. The danger of Frankenstein's ambition is reinforced by the violence and destruction that his ambition causes through the monster, and by the deterioration of Frankenstein's health throughout the rest of the novel.

Start by introducing the main point of your paragraph.

Use evidence from the extract to back up your point.

Explain how your evidence supports your original point.

Finally, develop your point by showing how it links to the rest of the text.

Worked Answer

Link your points to the novel's context and themes

Here's a point you could make about how Shelley uses <u>setting</u> to show the <u>dangers</u> of ambition:

> Shelley uses setting to highlight how dangerous ambition can be. Walton's ambition takes him to the Arctic, which is a hazardous environment that endangers the lives of himself and his crew.

1) This paragraph <u>builds</u> on the idea that ambition is presented as dangerous.

2) However, you can improve it by <u>quoting</u> from the text and <u>developing</u> your points:

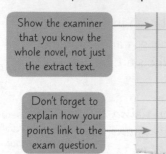

Show the examiner that you know the whole novel, not just the extract text.

Don't forget to explain how your points link to the exam question.

> In Walton's narrative, Shelley uses setting to highlight how dangerous it can be to pursue ambition. Walton travels to the Arctic, where he and his crew become "surrounded" by "mountains of ice" that threaten to "crush" his ship. The Arctic setting that Walton's "mad schemes" have brought him to is presented as full of danger, and pursuing his ambition has led to the death of "many" of his "unfortunate comrades". Walton's voyage builds upon Shelley's presentation of ambition as dangerous.

3) You could develop this by focusing on the <u>context</u> in which the novel was written:

> At the time in which Shelley was writing 'Frankenstein', the British government was planning two expeditions to the Arctic, and many explorers had already tried and failed to find a passage through the Arctic seas. Shelley's readers would have understood that a voyage like Walton's was incredibly dangerous, so Shelley uses Walton's expedition to highlight the danger that selfish ambition can lead to. Even in the face of terrible conditions, Walton struggles to let go of his ambition and allow his crew to turn around.

Make sure your comments on context are linked closely to the text and the question.

Finish your essay in style

You could say:

> In conclusion, 'Frankenstein' presents ambition as a dangerous thing, that should not be followed selfishly or obsessively. Shelley uses setting and violent imagery to emphasise this.

1) This conclusion is okay, but it doesn't <u>summarise</u> the points of the essay very well.

2) So to make it really <u>impressive</u> you could say something like...

> Ambition is clearly presented as dangerous when it's obsessively and selfishly pursued. It causes Frankenstein to suffer ill health, and the deaths of those he loves, and it causes Walton to endanger the lives of everyone on his ship. Shelley also uses violent imagery and setting to reinforce the idea that ambition is dangerous. To an extent, Shelley does show through Clerval's character that ambition does not have to be dangerous if it is moderated. However, the characters of Frankenstein and Walton are a clear warning against the obsessive pursuit of selfish ambition.

This shows that you've considered all the techniques Shelley used.

Make your last sentence really stand out — it's your last opportunity to impress the examiner.

Why do alligators write good essays? Their quotes are so snappy...

It seems like there's a lot to remember on these two pages, but there's not really. To summarise — write a scorching intro and a sizzling conclusion, make a good range of points (one per paragraph) and include plenty of examples. Easy.

Index

Index

The Characters in 'Frankenstein'

Phew! You should be an expert on *Frankenstein* by now. But if you want a bit of light relief and a quick recap of the novel's plot, sit yourself down and read through *Frankenstein — The Cartoon...*

Victor
Frankenstein

As a child

Monster

Robert
Walton

Elizabeth
Lavenza

As a child

Henry
Clerval

Alphonse
Frankenstein

Justine Moritz

Mary Shelley's 'Frankenstein'